# GREAT LIVES OBSERVED

Gerald Emanuel Stearn, *General Editor*

EACH VOLUME IN THE SERIES VIEWS THE CHARACTER AND ACHIEVEMENT OF A GREAT WORLD FIGURE IN THREE PERSPECTIVES—THROUGH HIS OWN WORDS, THROUGH THE OPINIONS OF HIS CONTEMPORARIES, AND THROUGH RETROSPECTIVE JUDGMENTS—THUS COMBINING THE INTIMACY OF AUTOBIOGRAPHY, THE IMMEDIACY OF EYEWITNESS OBSERVATION, AND THE OBJECTIVITY OF MODERN SCHOLARSHIP.

EMMA LOU THORNBROUGH, *Professor of History at Butler University, is a frequent contributor to several journals of history. She is also the author of* T. Thomas Fortune: Militant Journalist *and the editor of* Booker T. Washington, *another volume in the* Great Lives Observed *series.*

# BLACK RECONSTRUCTIONISTS

**Edited by**
**EMMA LOU THORNBROUGH**

*We feel that we are part and parcel of this great nation;
and as such . . . we propose to stay here and solve this
problem of whether the black race and the white race can
live together in this country.*

—RICHARD H. CAIN
(Speech to the 43rd Congress, 1874)

A SPECTRUM BOOK

PRENTICE-HALL, INC., ENGLEWOOD CLIFFS, N.J.

*Library of Congress Cataloging in Publication Data*

THORNBROUGH, EMMA LOU, comp.
   Black reconstructionists.

   (Great lives observed)   (A Spectrum Book)
   Includes bibliographical references.
     1. Reconstruction—Addresses, essays, lectures.
2. Negroes—Politics and suffrage—Southern States—
Addresses, essays, lectures.  I. Title.
E668.T48     322.1′19′6073075     72–4815
ISBN  0–13–077255–0
ISBN  0–13–077248–8 (pbk.)

PRENTICE-HALL INTERNATIONAL, INC. (*London*)
PRENTICE-HALL OF AUSTRALIA PTY. LTD. (*Sydney*)
PRENTICE-HALL OF CANADA LTD. (*Toronto*)
PRENTICE-HALL OF INDIA PRIVATE LIMITED (*New Delhi*)
PRENTICE-HALL OF JAPAN, INC. (*Tokyo*)

# Contents

PART ONE

**BLACK RECONSTRUCTIONISTS LOOK AT THE WORLD**

## 1

## 2

## 3

## 4

## 5

# 6

## Mississippi                                                          45

Robert Gleed, *45*   Hiram R. Revels, *47*   John R. Lynch, *48*

# 7

## South Carolina                                                      51

Beverly Nash, *51*   Robert C. DeLarge, *52*   Debates in the Constitutional Convention of 1868, *52*   Francis L. Cardozo speaks on the corruption issue, *59*   Blacks protest the Hamburg "riot," *61*

# 8

## Black Congressmen Speak                                             64

Demand protection of loyal men in the South, *64*   Civil rights, *67*   Richard H. Cain replies to a white congressman, *70*

## PART TWO
# THE WHITE WORLD LOOKS AT THE BLACK RECONSTRUCTIONISTS

# 9

## Southern Whites                                                     73

Georgia, *73*   Louisiana, *76*   Mississippi, *79*   South Carolina, *83*

# 10

## Members of Congress Look at Black Reconstructionists                89

Members debate the seating of the first black senator, *89* Congressmen debate the Sumner Civil Rights Bill, *91* Minority Report of the Ku Klux Klan Committee, *95*

GREAT LIVES OBSERVED

# BLACK
# RECONSTRUCTIONISTS

# Introduction

The most unprecedented and most revolutionary experiment of so-called "Radical" Reconstruction was the participation in politics by Southern blacks, most of whom were recently emancipated slaves. The sudden emergence into positions of leadership and responsibility by members of an oppressed race was a remarkable and exciting development, but one which has not received thorough study by historians.

Less than two years after the end of the Civil War, Congress provided by the Reconstruction Act of March 2, 1867, that new constitutions should be framed in the former Confederate states (except Tennessee[1]) by conventions of delegates elected by male citizens "of whatever race, color or previous condition." The constitutions were to give the right to vote to all who were eligible to vote for delegates to the conventions. Early in 1870, the Fifteenth Amendment to the U. S. Constitution, which declared that the right to vote should not be denied because of race, color, or previous condition of servitude, was ratified. These measures, which guaranteed political rights to blacks, were adopted in part to insure loyal governments in the South, in part to give blacks a protective weapon, and in part to insure the supremacy of the Republican party.

In the registration of voters under the Reconstruction Acts, from which some whites were excluded because of their support of the Confederate rebellion, the total number of whites registered was approximately 600,000; the total number of Negroes about 703,400. In Alabama, Florida, Louisiana, Mississippi, and South Carolina, black registrants outnumbered whites. In Georgia, the numbers of blacks and whites were about equal. The 1870 figures of the U. S. census showed blacks outnumbered whites in the total population in South Carolina, Mississippi, and Louisiana. In Alabama, Georgia, and Florida, the black population was at least four-fifths as large as the white. Black delegates were elected to all of the

1. The Reconstruction Act did not apply to Tennessee because that state had already ratified the Fourteenth Amendment and had been restored to the Union. The other former Confederate States had refused to ratify the Fourteenth Amendment and in consequence Congress enacted the Reconstruction Act.

1

state constitutional conventions which met in 1867–68, but only in South Carolina were they in a majority (76 of a total of 124). In Louisiana, half the delegates were black; in Mississippi, 17 of 100; in Georgia, 33 of 170; in Florida, 18 of 45; in Alabama, 18 of 108. In other states, where the percentage of blacks in the population was less, the number in the conventions was smaller than in the above-mentioned states.

Blacks were elected to all of the state legislatures after the new constitutions were ratified. In the first legislature in South Carolina, there were 87 Negroes and 40 whites. Negroes outnumbered whites in the lower house, but whites were in a majority in the upper house. In no other state did blacks ever constitute a majority in either house of the legislature, and in no other state was the percentage of blacks commensurate with their numbers in the total population. At the state level, a total of six blacks served as lieutenant governors, but no black was ever elected governor. One state supreme court justice was black, and in some states a few blacks were in administrative positions, including that of secretary of state, state treasurer, and superintendent of public instruction. Many more held such positions as justice of peace, sheriff, and alderman, at the county and city level. Between 1869 and 1880, a total of 16 Negroes served in Congress—two in the Senate, 14 in the House of Representatives.

In South Carolina, where they outnumbered whites 415,814 to 289,667 in 1870, blacks exercised the greatest political power and held the largest number of offices. South Carolina sent more blacks to Congress than any other state. There was no single pre-eminent black leader, but a number of able and influential figures emerged. Nearly all of them had a part in the founding of the Republican party in the state, and served an apprenticeship in the 1868 constitutional convention. One of the foremost was Robert Brown Elliott, a lawyer of great intellectual powers and oratorical ability, and an adroit politician, who was powerful in the Republican state organization and gained a national reputation. After serving in the state legislature and as assistant adjutant general of the state militia, he was twice elected to Congress. Evidently feeling he could do more for his personal fortune and for his race at home, however, he resigned and returned to South Carolina to become speaker of the lower house of the state legislature. In 1876, he was elected attorney general, but was forced to give up the office when President Hayes withdrew federal support from the Republican regime.

Less brilliant but of more enduring influence was Robert Smalls, who was elected to Congress five times. He continued to represent the Beaufort district, which contained the highest ratio of blacks, after the white counter-revolution had swept the rest of the state. Today, Smalls would be called a successful "ethnic" leader, who understood and identified with the aspirations of his black constituents and sought tangible gains for them. As a member of the constitutional convention of 1895, Smalls made a powerful though futile protest against the Tillman disfranchisement movement.

A natural leader and a self-assertive, experienced orator was Richard H. Cain, a minister of the African Methodist Episcopal Church, popularly known as "Daddy" Cain. He had great power among the Negroes in the Charleston area, where his church was considered one of the strongest political organizations in the state. The *Missionary Record,* which he ably edited, exerted political as well as religious influence. After serving in the state senate, he went to Washington as congressman-at-large, where he made good use of his oratorical talents, especially in challenging white racist colleagues.

Joseph H. Rainey of Georgetown, elected five times to the House of Representatives, served longer in Congress than any other black member during Reconstruction. Alonzo J. Ransier of Charleston, who served one term in Congress (1873–75), had previously been chairman of the State Republican Central Committee and lieutenant governor. Robert DeLarge was active in founding the Republican party in South Carolina, served in the constitutional convention of 1868, the state legislature, and as state land commissioner before being elected, in 1870, to Congress, where he served for one term.

Two able blacks who held positions of responsibility at the state level were Jonathan Jasper Wright of Beaufort and Francis L. Cardozo of Charleston. The former, a native of Pennsylvania and the first Negro admitted to the bar in that state, was elected by the South Carolina legislature to the state supreme court. Cardozo, a native South Carolinian, who had been educated at the University of Glasgow and at Presbyterian seminaries in Edinburgh and London, and had been pastor of the Temple Congregational church in New Haven, Connecticut, returned to Charleston, in 1865 (at the request of the American Missionary Association), to found a school for Negro boys. Later, he served capably as secretary of state and state treasurer. Even whites testified as to his probity. Richard H. Gleaves, a native of Pennsylvania, who became a business partner of Robert Smalls at Beaufort, was elected lieutenant governor in 1872. He presided capably over the state senate, but on the whole seems to have had little influence.

Many other blacks who held lesser offices showed capacity for leadership. Two outstanding examples were Beverly Nash and Prince Rivers. The former, an exslave and hotel waiter, who became owner of a coal yard, was a power in the Republican state organization and in the legislature. Rivers, who had been a coachman in Beaufort, as a member of the black regiment which Thomas Wentworth Higginson commanded, so impressed Higginson that he declared that if there were ever a black monarchy in South Carolina, Rivers would be its king. Later, in the state legislature, Rivers commanded a loyal following of black members. He was an important Republican leader in the Hamburg area and a major general in the state militia.

Although blacks made up the vast majority of Republican voters in Mississippi—the 1870 census showed 444,201 blacks and 382,896 whites—they did not obtain as many important offices as in South Carolina. Three of the best-known black Reconstructionists, however, were Mississippians—Hiram H. Revels, a minister of the African Methodist Episcopal church, the first black member of the United States Senate, elected to fill the unexpired term of Jefferson Davis; Blanche K. Bruce, who served a full six-year term in the Senate; and John R. Lynch, who was three times elected to the U. S. House of Representatives. Revels, who entered the political arena reluctantly, was an eminently respectable member of the Senate; he was rather diffident, however, and so eager to win the good will of whites that he probably had little enthusiastic support from the masses of his own race. Bruce, who was a planter and a man of distinguished appearance, associated easily with white colleagues in the Senate, but was not aggressive. Far more of a leader was Lynch, who helped organize the Republican party in Mississippi before he was old enough to vote, was appointed a justice of peace at twenty-one, and was speaker of the state house of representatives at twenty-four. The next year, he went to Congress.

Perhaps an even more dynamic figure, but less well-known than John R. Lynch (a self-educated former slave), was James D. Lynch, an educated black clergyman from Pennsylvania, who was elected secretary of state in 1869—the first black elected to state office in Mississippi. He was idolized by the black masses and respected by white Republicans. James Hill, a former slave, who also served capably as secretary of state, had a large following and was probably more influential in state politics than Bruce or John R. Lynch. A. K. Davis, a rather obscure figure who was elected lieutenant governor in 1874, was evidently a weak man with little capacity as a leader. Thomas W. Cardozo had educational attainments that qualified him to become superintendent of education, but apparently was ineffectual and probably dishonest.

The story of Reconstruction in Louisiana is more complex than in any other state and, for this reason, perhaps, few scholars have attempted to deal with it. Census figures show Negroes and mulattoes in a slight majority, but the race situation was complicated by the high percentage of persons of mixed blood. From the records it is impossible, for example, to determine accurately how many members of the state legislature were classified as "colored." Before the war, there had been a large, free, colored population in New Orleans that could be expected to furnish leadership after emancipation. During Reconstruction, a number of able black leaders emerged, some of them natives, others from outside the state. Three of them attained the office of lieutenant governor: Oscar J. Dunn (1868–71); Pinckney B. S. Pinchback (1871–72); and C. C. Antoine (1872–76). Other state officers were P. G. Deslonde, secretary of state; Antoine Dubuclet, state treasurer; and W. G. Brown, superintendent of public education. J. Willis Menard, of New Orleans, was the first black man certified as having been elected to the U. S. House of Representatives, but his white opponent contested the election, and the House failed to seat either man. Charles E. Nash, elected to the House of Representatives in 1874, was the only Louisiana black who actually served in Congress.

Dunn and Pinchback, by far the most important of the group, presented a sharp contrast. Dunn, the first black to be elected to a high administrative post in any state, was a full-blooded Negro—a slave who had emancipated himself at an early age by running away. He was a plasterer by trade, but had also learned enough of violin-playing to give lessons. A man of great native ability, courage, and integrity, Dunn was incorruptible, even in the eyes of whites. He became critical of Governor Henry C. Warmoth, his white carpetbagger colleague, and attempted to lead a revolt against him, but died suddenly, in 1871.

Pinchback, the most influential and adroit of Louisiana blacks, could easily have passed for white. He was the son of a slave mother and a white Mississippi planter, who had taken the mother and her children north to free them. After the death of the father, his relatives attempted to re-enslave them. Young Pinchback escaped and went to work on river boats on the Mississippi River. He arrived in New Orleans soon after Union troops had occupied it and began recruiting for the Corps D'Afrique. A seasoned politician who had been a member of the constitutional convention and the legislature, he became lieutenant governor after Dunn's death. In the rapidly shifting alliances of the period he was sometimes on the side of Warmoth, sometimes opposed to him. When the governor was impeached in December, 1872, Pinchback was acting governor for a few weeks. Thereafter, he was elected by the legislature to the U. S. Senate, but was never seated. After four years of delay, the Senate decided by a vote of 32 to 29 that his election had been illegal.

In Georgia, where there were about five blacks to every six whites, blacks had little influence in the Republican party and won few offices. The 3 blacks elected to the state senate and the 29 elected to the lower house after the adoption of the 1868 constitution were expelled on the grounds that the constitution gave Negroes the right to vote but not to hold office. The black members were eventually reinstated, but only after Congress had temporarily restored military rule in Georgia.

One of the members expelled was Henry M. Turner, a man much hated by white Georgians but one of the most remarkable of the black Reconstructionists. A minister of the African Methodist Episcopal church who was serving in Washington, D. C. during the Civil War, he had been an early advocate of the use of black troops, insisting that the war could not be won without them. The first black chaplain commissioned by Lincoln, he came to Georgia as a chaplain with the Freedmen's Bureau and was soon educating the freedmen for political action. He played an important part in establishing the Republican party in the state, and was a member of the constitutional convention. His experience at the hands of the white politicians in the legislature embittered him. He warned his black colleagues not to trust white men and not to fight for a country that refused to recognize their rights. In the post-Reconstruction era, as a bishop of the African Methodist Episcopal church, he became the most influential advocate of the back-to-Africa movement of the 1890s. Turner was the outstanding black leader in Georgia, but there were other able blacks in the legislature. One of them, Jefferson Long of Macon, was elected to the U. S. House of Representatives in 1870, but his tenure was too short to give him an opportunity to accomplish anything.

In Alabama, the black-white ratio in population was about the same as in Georgia; as in Georgia, although Negroes constituted more than ninety percent of the membership of the Republican party, they were given few offices. The hostility of the white population and the rural character of most of the black population militated against the development of black leadership. In the constitutional convention of 1867, there were 18 blacks out of a total of 90 delegates. In the first legislature, there were 26 blacks out of a total membership of 84. No black was elected to a state office in Alabama, but three were elected to Congress. Of these, the most important was James T. Rapier of Florence, son of a white planter and a free black mother. Educated by private tutors and at the University of Glasgow and Montreal College, he was a scholar and a successful planter. He was a member of the constitutional convention, a member of the committee that wrote the state's first Republican platform, and Republican candidate for secretary of state in 1870 (defeated along with the rest of the ticket). In 1872, he was elected to Congress, where he became one of the most effective advocates of Sumner's Civil Rights Bill. Renominated in 1874, he was defeated by a Democrat. Benjamin Sterling Turner of Selma, a former slave, was a member of the Forty-second Congress (1871–73). Exslave Jeremiah Haralson, a self-educated farmer, was a member of the Forty-fourth Congress (1875–77). A white newspaper described Haralson as "uncompromising, irritating, bold," but he favored a general amnesty and opposed the use of federal troops to protect black voters—thereby arousing misgivings among some of his black constituents.

In Florida, the newest and least populous of the former Confederate states, whites outnumbered blacks by less than 5,000. In the constitutional convention of 1868, there were 18 black delegates out of a total of 45. In the first legislature, 19 of 76 members were black. A number of these men were able, but blacks received few important offices. Nevertheless, for a time, Florida's one member in the U. S. House of Representatives was a black—Josiah T. Walls. Walls, who had an impressive Civil War record, had come to Florida as a sergeant in the Union army and remained to become a successful farmer. He was elected to Congress in 1870, after serving in the constitutional convention and the state legislature. After redistricting gave Florida two seats in the House, he was elected in 1872 and 1874. Two of these elections (1870 and 1874) were contested by Democrats; in both cases, Walls was ultimately unseated after serving most of his term. It was generally agreed, however, that he was a capable congressman, who conscientiously sought to represent the interests of all his constituents, regardless of race.

In state politics, the most able black was Jonathan Gibbs, who was born in Philadelphia, graduated from Dartmouth College, and attended Princeton Theological Seminary, before entering the Presbyterian ministry. He went south after the war to do missionary work among the freedmen. After enfranchisement, he decided he could best serve his race in the secular field. Probably the best educated member of the constitutional convention of 1868, he was a trusted and influential member of the cabinet of Governor Harrison Reed, who appointed him secretary of state. In 1873, he was made superintendent of public instruction, but died suddenly in 1874.

In Virginia, where the percentage of blacks was about as great as in Georgia and Alabama, blacks had even less political power. In North Carolina, Arkansas, and Texas, the ratio of blacks to whites was smaller. The constitutional conventions and legislatures of all these states had capable black members, but conditions did not give them an opportunity to become influential leaders.

Of the black Reconstructionists, only John R. Lynch published his memoirs, and few personal papers of any of them survive. Most accounts by contemporary whites are extremely biased, and white writers in general tended to treat black politicians as a stereotyped group, rather than as individuals with distinct backgrounds and personalities. Thus, the paucity of records and the nature of those that survive make it difficult, and sometimes impossible, for the present-day historian to reconstruct details of the lives of most of these men. But enough information is available to destroy some of the stereotypes. It is impossible to draw a composite portrait of a "typical" black Reconstructionist. Some were native Southerners; others were black carpetbaggers from the North. Some were ex-slaves; others were freeborn. Many were of mixed blood; others were pure black. Their educational and economic backgrounds varied.

It is also impossible to make an accurate estimate of how many black Reconstructionists were former slaves. Some of the better-known were freeborn, but of the 16 black congressmen, 10 had been slaves. Only Revels, Walls, Ransier, Elliott, Cain, and Rapier were freeborn. Of the 74 black delegates in the South Carolina constitutional convention, 38 were certainly slaves, and the status of some of the others is not known. Probably the proportions of slaves in other conventions were similar. Among blacks holding local offices, the percentage of former slaves was high, and undoubtedly some were illiterate. But many of the leaders born into slavery managed to educate themselves and to become businessmen or skilled artisans, or even practice law. Others were teachers or preachers. It appears that Joel Williamson's comment about South Carolina is true of other states as well: "The one thing that most native Negro leaders were not was fresh from the cotton fields." [2]

Slaves who were the sons of white masters enjoyed opportunities usually denied slaves. Most of them were more white than black in ancestry, and some could easily have "passed" into white society had they chosen to do so. W. E. B. Du Bois described Pinchback as, "to all intents and purposes . . . an educated, well-to-do, congenial white man, with but a few drops of Negro blood, which he did not stoop to deny, as so many of his fellow whites did." [3] Theophile T. Allain, another Republican leader in Louisiana and member of the legislature, who was the son of a white sugar planter, traveled in Europe with his father and was sent to a private school in New Jersey. Blanche K. Bruce was the son of a favorite household slave and a white master. As a boy he received unusual advantages, sharing a tutor with his young master. He emancipated himself early in the war, took service on a river boat, ultimately settled in Bolivar County, Mississippi, and soon was a successful planter and sheriff

2. Joel Williamson, *After Slavery: The Negro in South Carolina During Reconstruction, 1861–1877* (Chapel Hill, N. C.: University of North Carolina Press, 1965), p. 376.

3. W. E. B. Du Bois, *Black Reconstruction in America* (New York: Russell and Russell, 1935; reprinted by Atheneum, 1969), p. 469.

of the county. John R. Lynch was the son of a wealthy white Louisiana father, who had written instructions that his slave wife and her children were to be freed in the event of his death. But they were sold and sent to Natchez, Mississippi. There young John managed to educate himself and learn the photographer's trade.

Francis L. Cardozo was the son of a white father; and, as we have already seen, Rapier, who was freeborn, also had a white father. Numerous other black Reconstructionists of predominantly white ancestry could be mentioned. Other leaders, however, were pure black or nearly so. Outstanding among them was Robert Brown Elliott, who was very dark in color. Frederick Douglass, who greatly admired Elliott's intellectual powers, said that there was no doubt as to his complexion or features. "To all outward seeming, he might have been an ordinary Negro, one might have delved . . . with spade and pickaxe." Freeborn Jonathan J. Wright was pure black as were also exslaves Beverly Nash and Prince Rivers. Among the Louisiana leaders, Oscar Dunn was all-black as was C. C. Antoine, who boasted that his grandfather was an African chief. Nash, Louisiana's only Negro congressman, was all-black as was Alabama congressman Haralson, who used this fact to win black votes in a political contest with the light-skinned Rapier.

Many of the black Reconstructionists were carpetbaggers—men from the North, like Jonathan Wright and Jonathan Gibbs, who came to the South during or immediately after the war. In a number of cases, they were freeborn southerners who had moved to the free states. Revels, son of a free black Baptist preacher and a Scottish mother, was born in North Carolina but went north to study and preach. Henry M. Turner was born in South Carolina, the son of a free black father and a German mother. He had been sent to Baltimore for pastoral training. Richard H. Cain, the son of a free black father and a Cherokee Indian mother, was born in Virginia but taken to Ohio as a child.

Obviously, the stereotype of the illiterate, gullible field-hand-legislator or congressman was false. In spite of the obstacles imposed by law in both free and slave states, most of the black leaders had obtained a basic education. Many were largely self-taught, as were many of the white leaders of the period, including Andrew Johnson. A few had superior educational attainments. Cardozo, Gibbs, and Rapier have already been mentioned. Revels had attended Knox College for one year; Cain had been at Wilberforce

College for one year; Bruce had attended the preparatory department at Oberlin. Elliott claimed to have studied at High Holborn Academy and Eton College in England and to have read law in London; recent research has cast doubt on these claims, but no one doubts that he was an able, even brilliant lawyer, who was said to own one of the best law libraries in South Carolina and to have a knowledge of several languages. As already mentioned, Wright was the first Negro admitted to the bar in Pennsylvania. Lynch was also a lawyer who practiced for many years in Chicago after leaving Mississippi.

The economic conditions of the black leaders varied as greatly as their educational backgrounds. In an age that glorified the self-made man, some black Reconstructionists who began life as slaves amassed fortunes; others lived in humble circumstances. Some were artisans or farmers of modest means. Oscar Dunn was a plasterer; Alonzo Rainey, a barber; Charles E. Nash, a bricklayer; Jefferson Long, a tailor; Benjamin S. Turner, a liveryman; Alonzo J. Ransier, a shipping clerk. DeLarge was a small farmer; Walls was a successful truck farmer. Blanche K. Bruce, Lynch, and Rapier all owned plantations. Robert Smalls was able to acquire extensive holdings of real estate in Beaufort and vicinity when property was offered for sale at government tax auctions. From business activities and other sources, Pinchback acquired stocks and bonds that yielded an income of ten thousand dollars a year. Elliott was reputed to be worth a hundred thousand dollars by the time he was first elected to Congress (money received, according to his political enemies, from railroads for services he rendered as a member of the state legislature).

One characteristic many black Reconstructionists shared was their youth. Lynch, who was speaker of the Mississippi House of Representatives at twenty-four, was the most striking example, but Bruce, Elliott, DeLarge, Rapier, Haralson, and Walls were still in their twenties when first elected to public office. Pinchback, Smalls, and Henry M. Turner were slightly older, while Cain and Revels were in their forties before becoming politically active.

By what avenues did these men of varied backgrounds and opportunities rise to positions of influence and responsibility? For many, service in the armed forces of the Union was preparation for leadership. The most celebrated example was Robert Smalls, the South Carolina slave-pilot who absconded with the Confederate vessel,

*Planter,* and delivered it and its cargo of guns and ammunition to the Union Navy. For this and other services, he was eventually given the rank of captain. As a recruiter of Negro troops, Pinchback won the rank of captain. Congressman Nash, who lost an arm in combat, was a major sergeant in the *Chasseurs D'Afrique.* Walls also had a good combat record and the rank of sergeant. Many lesser figures, such as Prince Rivers, also served in the Union Army.

Many black Reconstructionists, including some of the Union soldiers, entered politics via their work in the Freedmen's Bureau. Some were Bureau agents, others were teachers in schools sponsored by the Bureau. Jonathan Wright came to South Carolina as a legal adviser to the Bureau. William J. Whipper, a native of Michigan, served in the Union Army in South Carolina, became a Bureau agent, then a member of the constitutional convention and the legislature. Congressman DeLarge, a native South Carolinian, was also a Bureau agent. Many other examples could be given.

Probably the largest single group of leaders were ministers. Jonathan Gibbs and Francis L. Cardozo were Presbyterian and Congregational ministers respectively, but the most conspicuous examples of minister-politicians were found in the African Methodist Episcopal church. Hiram Revels preferred the ministry to politics, but Richard H. Cain, Henry M. Turner, and James D. Lynch combined religious and political careers with enthusiasm. Many lesser black leaders were preachers in either the African Methodist Episcopal church or Baptist churches.

All black Reconstructionists of any stature were Republicans. This is not surprising, since Republicans had taken the lead in the movement for civil and political rights for blacks, which Democrats had consistently opposed. White Republicans organized Union Leagues, educated blacks in the fundamentals of politics, actively sought their votes, and gave them some voice in party affairs and a share of the offices. Democrats, on the other hand, blatantly championed white supremacy. When they sought black votes, it was frequently by threatening reprisals for failure to support them, rather than by promising rewards. Democrats often asserted that the former master class was the freedman's best friend, and that if left to themselves without the interference of outsiders, the former slaves would have voted Democratic; but there is little evidence to support these claims. Blacks sometimes voted for Democrats, often under duress; occasionally a black leader might urge the support of a Democrat to defeat an objectionable Republican, but no leader of any standing was ever identified with the Democrats. After a few years, many blacks became disillusioned by the treatment they received from white Republican leaders, especially by their failure to give blacks, who in many places made up more than 90 percent of the Republican vote, a larger share of offices. But they continued to serve the GOP loyally, even after national leaders had deserted them.

In the constitutional conventions, blacks, with few exceptions, supported universal suffrage. They regarded the right to vote as a necessary weapon for defending their rights and improving their condition. On the whole, they were remarkably magnanimous toward whites, and seldom tried to limit the rights of former Confederates. But in Congress, especially after the rise of the Ku Klux Klan, some black members opposed a general amnesty on the grounds that disloyalty and disobedience to the Constitution were still rampant. Generally, black Reconstructionists strongly supported intervention by the federal government to protect blacks in the exercise of political rights.

Probably the greatest and most lasting achievement of the black Reconstructionists was their part in the establishment of public school systems. In the constitutional conventions and legislatures, they were unanimous in support of measures to make schools available to all children, but not all of them agreed that attendance should be compulsory. There were also some differences over the question of whether or not separate schools for black and white children should be permitted.

Historians agree that for the mass of exslaves land took priority over every other issue. Many of the newly enfranchised black voters hoped and expected that plantations of exmasters would be confiscated. Although black leaders agreed as to the importance of land, none favored confiscation, and they did little to promote measures to enable freedmen to become independent farmers. The one exception was in South Carolina. The 1868 constitutional convention, with the assent of the black members, declared: "The only manner in which any land can be obtained by the landless will be to purchase it." Nevertheless, it created a land commission empowered to buy land, subdivide it into small plots, and sell it at cost, plus interest, to farmers, who paid for it over a number of years.

Blacks wanted to abolish all legal disabilities and distinctions based on race. Many advocated legislation to penalize discrimination in public accommodations. Black congressmen, who knew from personal experience the humiliation and discomforts to which blacks who traveled were subjected, were strong supporters of Sumner's Civil Rights Bill. At the same time, most were careful to assure white colleagues that they did not seek "social equality." While denying any desire for interracial marriages, blacks nevertheless regarded anti-miscegenation laws as an affront. Sometimes, as in the Arkansas constitutional convention, they pointed out that under the slave system, white men had been responsible for whatever race-mixing there was.

Diffident and inexperienced, some black members of constitutional conventions and state legislatures said little and tended to follow the leadership of whites. But others initiated measures and debated actively and intelligently. Although they were a tiny minority and sometimes subjected to derogatory treatment by white colleagues, most black congressmen debated effectively and sometimes brilliantly, showing themselves quite capable of defending themselves and their race against disparagement by white members. As they gained political experience and sophistication, black leaders and their constituents demanded a larger voice in the Republican party and a larger share of offices.

From the beginning, it was clear that large numbers of southern whites intended to resist, by any means at their command, legal and political equality for former slaves. In the interval of presidential Reconstruction immediately following the war, state legislatures enacted the notorious "black codes," defining and circumscribing the rights of freedmen. As the specter of Negro suffrage became a reality, political conventions and other assemblages reiterated that this was a white man's government and called upon all whites to unite to resist "Negro domination," "Africanization," and "amalgamation" of the races. Many of these whites sought to prevent the ratification of the new constitutions with their provisions of universal suffrage by boycotting the referenda. Intimidation and violence to prevent Negroes from voting began at this time and continued to be a widely used tactic in many places henceforth. The transformation of the Ku Klux Klan from a social organization and its spread throughout the South and the rise of other organizations, secret and non-secret, which had as their purpose keeping Negroes in their "place," were the direct result of the enfranchisement of the blacks.

Emancipation intensified all the pathological race fears that had existed under slavery, and led to a revival and expansion of the methods of control used under slavery. As Allen Trelease observes in his recent massive and authoritative work, *White Terror: The Ku Klux Klan Conspiracy and Southern Reconstruction,* the Klan "institutionalized a white vigilantism which long preceded and followed it." [4] Klansmen and members of similar groups engaged in a variety of activities against blacks, such as punishing them for crimes or alleged crimes, or deterring them from committing crimes, and punishing blacks who were considered "insolent" or "uppity." Blacks who could read or write were likely to be considered insolent because of these attainments, and both blacks and whites who taught in Negro schools were considered especially objectionable. In many places, but especially in Mississippi, destruction of Negro schools and harassment of teachers were major Klan activities. But the supreme insolence was the exercise of recently granted political rights. The Klan and other groups resorted to intimidation, whippings, even murders, to prevent blacks from voting the Republican ticket and as reprisals for political activities on behalf of Republicans. Terrorism continued until the last Republican regime was overthrown and white supremacy was restored.

In some cases, whites deliberately fomented riots, which sometimes became massacres, and which had the intended effect of intimidating blacks from voting. Some black Reconstructionists were killed in cold blood. No major black leader was assassinated, but a number of minor office-holders were thus eliminated. For example, B. F. Randolph, a South Carolina state senator, who had come south as a chaplain to a Negro regiment and had later established a Negro school, was gunned down in broad daylight, on a railroad platform, by three members of a Democratic secret committee. At least two members of the South Carolina House of Representatives were murdered. In Louisiana, where there were mass murders during the 1868 Presidential campaign, one of the victims was a black member of the recent constitutional convention. Another active

4. Allen W. Trelease, *White Terror: The Ku Klux Klan Conspiracy and Southern Reconstruction* (New York: Harper and Row, 1971), p. xxii.

black Republican was dragged from his home, shot, and beheaded. In Alabama, the black president of a Grant and Colfax club was killed by an armed band when he refused to discontinue meetings. Many more local leaders were whipped or mutilated. Some of the whippings were carried out to compel blacks to promise to support Democratic candidates.

Blacks sometimes attacked whites, but in most cases violence was initiated by whites, although they asserted that they were acting in self-defense. Rumors of plots of armed uprisings by blacks were rife and were used by whites to justify repressive measures. When blacks attempted to defend themselves, they were likely to be overawed by the whites and were often compelled to surrender guns they had acquired for self-defense.

As the terror mounted, Republican officials called upon the federal government for protection. Congress responded by passing the Force Acts. In some areas where federal troops were sent, particularly in South Carolina, violence and intimidation were curbed, at least temporarily. But the Grant administration and Northern Republican leaders, aware of growing disenchantment in the North over Reconstruction policies, showed less and less inclination to intervene. State militia also failed to suppress violence.

The only troops Republican governors could trust were white unionists and blacks. The arming of blacks was regarded by most whites as the supreme insult; attempts to use black troops was countered by more violence by armed whites; the destruction of the black militia became one of the objectives of the white supremacists. Fear of wholesale bloodshed and race warfare prevented governors from calling out black militia, and their failure to take decisive action against white armed bands was an important factor in enabling white "Redeemers" to overthrow Republican regimes.

White Republicans, both native scalawags and carpetbaggers, defended the right of Negroes to vote, since white candidates were dependent upon black votes for election. But few whites were willing to give blacks offices or power commensurate with their numbers. Some whites, such as Governor Warmoth of Louisiana, expressed apprehension that some of the more militant black Republicans would seek to "Africanize" the government.

Black Reconstructionists elected to Congress were sometimes subjected to humiliating treatment by their white colleagues. When, in the House, John Harris of Virginia asserted, "I say there is not one gentleman upon this floor who can honestly say he really believes the colored man his equal," Alonzo Ransier said, "I can." Harris replied: "Of course you can; but I am speaking to the white men of the House." When Ransier objected again to his remarks, Harris said, "I do not allow you to interrupt me. Sit down; I am talking to white men; I am talking to gentlemen." On the other hand, some white members received their black colleagues with courtesy and applauded their speeches. Robert Brown Elliott's brilliant defense of the Civil Rights Bill was especially praised by Republican congressmen and in the Northern press.

The turbulent state of politics in the former Confederate states, the appeals by Republican officials for federal intervention to protect constitutional rights, and contested elections led to congressional investigations that amassed volume upon volume of testimony on political conditions in the South. By far the best known and most important is the report of the joint committee that investigated the activities of the Klan in 1871. The first of the thirteen volumes consisted of a majority report by the Republican members of the committee and a minority report by the Democrats. The majority concluded that Southern whites would have opposed any Reconstruction policy that included "the liberation, the civil and political elevation of the negro," and that the activities of the Ku Klux Klan and similar groups were fundamentally intended to deprive Negroes of their rights and overthrow Republican regimes.

The Democratic minority, in contrast, denied the existence of any conspiracy to resist the laws, minimized acts of violence by whites, and decried the "oppression" of the white South. "Negro-domination" and the alleged corruption and depravity of the Negro governments were emphasized. The language of the minority report, typical of much of the political rhetoric of white supremacist Democrats of the period, helped to perpetuate a legend about Reconstruction that influenced much later writing.

The novelty of participation of blacks in politics attracted attention from Northern journalists and foreign travelers. The observations of such men were likely to be superficial and to reflect their personal, political, and, especially, their racial prejudices. These writers, for the most part, treated black Reconstructionists *en masse* and had little to say about individuals. Apparently they did not even make an effort to interview any black legislators or state officials, although they recorded extensive conversations with whites.

During the Reconstruction years, a legend of "Negro domination" as an orgy of misrule and corruption developed—a legend that influenced historical scholarship for decades and that shows some vitality even today. The assumptions and the rhetoric of the minority report of the Ku Klux Klan committee, sensational journalistic accounts, such as James S. Pike's *Prostrate State,* and similar books were accepted at face value and incorporated into later accounts, both popular and scholarly.

The legend of misrule was given respectability by some of the most distinguished historians of the early twentieth century, among them James Ford Rhodes and John W. Burgess. Especially influential was the work of William A. Dunning of Columbia University. Under his direction a crop of Ph.D. candidates produced monographs on Reconstruction in the individual states of the South. All the members of the "Dunning School" were trained scholars who did intensive research in primary sources, but all wrote from the racist point of view of the period. All were sympathetic to the white South and doubtful of the capacity of blacks.

Meanwhile, black writers began to reassess Reconstruction. Especially significant and influential was the work of W. E. B. Du Bois. In 1909, at the meeting of the American Historical Association, he read a paper on "Reconstruction and Its Benefits," which was largely ignored at the time, but which was to influence later writers. Other black historians, such as Alrutheus A. Taylor, also published scholarly revisionist studies, but they attracted little attention. Indeed, whites appeared to prefer to cling to the legend. W. E. B. Du Bois tells us that when he submitted an article on the American Negro that he had been invited to write for the *Encyclopædia Britannica* he included a paragraph on Reconstruction in which he said that Negroes believed that Negro votes were responsible for restoring the South to the Union and for establishing democracy and public schools in the South. The editors insisted upon deleting the paragraph, and Du Bois refused to permit publication of the article without it. In 1935, Du Bois published *Black Reconstruction in America, 1860–1880,* a full-scale review and reinterpretation emphasizing the role of blacks and the bias of earlier writers.

By the 1930s, white scholars had begun to take a new look at Reconstruction. The publication, in 1932, of *Reconstruction in South Carolina*, by Francis L. Simkins and Robert H. Woody, was especially influential. Later, Vernon L. Wharton, Joe M. Richardson, and Joel Williamson published monographs on Mississippi, Florida, and South Carolina respectively, which contributed significantly to destroying old myths, throwing new light on the role of blacks in Reconstruction, and detailing the careers of some of the black leaders. Other more general studies (notably *Reconstruction After the Civil War*, by the distinguished black historian, John Hope Franklin) have helped to revise the traditional view of black Reconstructionists. Few writers, however, have written biographies of the black leaders. Samuel Denny Smith and Maurine Christopher have published collective biographies of black members of Congress. A few sketches of other black leaders have been published in scholarly journals, and some popular biographies written especially for children have appeared. But Okon Edet Uya's biography of Robert Smalls, published in 1971, was the first significant, scholarly, book-length study of a black Reconstructionist.[5]

In spite of increased research and revised interpretations of black Reconstruction, there remain important questions about the black Reconstructionists themselves, to which only tentative answers can be given. One such question concerns the extent to which the leaders (who were usually men of some means and frequently of mixed blood) really expressed the aspirations of the black masses. There is abundant evidence that for most freedmen the great *desideratum* was land. But, as we have seen, black leaders rejected confiscation and showed little interest in any proposals for measures to assist freedmen in buying land or other economic measures in their behalf. More than half a century ago, W. E. B. Du Bois said that to give Negroes the vote "without land as an economic underpinning" was merely "to end a civil war by beginning a race feud." Many historians today would agree. Perhaps the most serious fault that can be charged against the black Reconstructionists was their failure to fight vigorously for measures to enable former slaves to become independent farmers instead of sharecroppers. It is evident from their published speeches that, like their white contemporaries, they subscribed to the tenets of *laissez-faire* economics and the sanctity of private property, and therefore opposed confiscation and

5. See Bibliographical Note, pp. 171–72, for other books and articles.

government aid. Many of them were successful, "self-made" men, who had surmounted poverty through their own initiative and good luck, and who probably thought similar opportunities were available to other blacks. Perhaps also, as political realists, black Reconstructionists recognized that it was futile to press for anything as revolutionary as land confiscation or large-scale government aid and that to do so would simply alienate white allies. Black leaders who tended to identify with white colleagues on economic issues were, nevertheless, nearly always assertive and uncompromising in their demands for guarantees of civil and political rights.

Another question that needs to be explored more fully is the relationship of black and white political leaders and the attitudes of black voters to white leaders. Obviously, the black leaders and their constituents were not a monolithic group; attitudes varied among them; but certain trends are discernible. Initially, newly enfranchised blacks were ready to accept white leadership and asked for few offices for blacks. Black leaders, publicly at least, nearly always adopted a conciliatory attitude toward whites, and stressed the mutuality of interests of the two races. Some of them said openly that blacks should be modest in their demands until they had gained experience and demonstrated their capacity. But after a few years, blacks, who made up the vast majority of Republican voters in many places, began to reject the role of passive supporters of white leaders and to become more assertive. Under pressure from the rank and file, black leaders began to demand a larger voice in the Republican party and more offices, even though some of them recognized that this would alienate whites from the party.

A final question, to which again only tentative answers can be given, is why black leaders did not make more vigorous and aggressive efforts to resist violence and intimidation. Could they have done anything effective to prevent the overthrow of the Reconstruction governments? As already seen, black leaders consistently and repeatedly urged federal intervention, but on the whole, actions by the federal government were too little and too late. White governors hesitated to use militia units made up principally of blacks, apparently because of fear of aggravating white violence and race conflict. Black leaders, however, do not appear to have offered any serious challenge to the governors on this point. There were numerous instances in which blacks forcibly resisted white assailants, and in some instances blacks initiated attacks on whites.

Black leaders denounced white violence in strong terms, but forcible resistance received little endorsement from them, no doubt because they feared that armed confrontation would be calamitous to the black community and would completely alienate white support. Evidence of the dilemma in which black leaders were caught, and the resulting ambivalence in their rhetoric, is found in the resolutions framed with the assistance of Richard H. Cain and other leaders, following the Hamburg Riot in South Carolina.[6] The resolutions declared that the Negro would not always be "docile," that the rising generation of blacks was "as brave and daring as white men," and hinted at the use of Winchester rifles; but it ended by stating that if the governor did not bring the white perpetrators of the riot to justice, the blacks must "peaceably assemble and petition the National Government through legal channels 'for redress of grievances.' "

Since emancipation, the black people of the South had learned much about politics and government and were developing racial solidarity and self-respect. But their very successes seemed to strengthen the determination of many whites to nullify their gains. Increased solidarity among blacks and evidence of increased political power stimulated white solidarity and caused whites to desert the Republican party. Faced with the defection of their white allies in the South, the indifference of former friends in the North, the failure of the Grant administration and the Southern Republican governors to take vigorous action, black leaders were caught in a cruel and seemingly impossible situation. Under the circumstances, there was probably no course of action open to them that could have stemmed the counter-revolution that overthrew the Reconstruction experiment.

6. The resolutions are printed below, pp. 62–63.

# Chronology

| | |
|---|---|
| **1865** | (December 18) Thirteenth Amendment |
| **1866** | (April 9) Civil Rights Act |
| **1867** | (March 2) First Reconstruction Act provides for registration of black voters |
| | (June) Republican convention in New Orleans promises equal treatment to blacks |
| | (July) Republican organizations including blacks organized in Mississippi and South Carolina |
| **1868** | (January 14) South Carolina Constitutional Convention meets |
| | (April) Oscar J. Dunn elected lieutenant governor of Louisiana |
| | (July 28) Fourteenth Amendment |
| **1870** | (January 20) Hiram Revels elected to U. S. Senate |
| | (February) Jasper J. Wright elected to South Carolina supreme court |
| | (March 30) Fifteenth Amendment |
| | (December 12) Joseph H. Rainey, first black member sworn in as member of U. S. House of Representatives |
| **1870–71** | Forty-first Congress—two black members in House |
| **1871–73** | Forty-second Congress—four black members in House |
| **1871** | (April 20) Act to Enforce Fourteenth Amendment (Ku Klux Klan Act) |
| **1872–73** | (December, 1872–January, 1873) P. B. S. Pinchback acting governor of Louisiana |
| **1872** | John R. Lynch Speaker of Mississippi House of Representatives |
| **1874** | (February 3) Blanche K. Bruce elected to U. S. Senate |
| **1873–75** | Forty-third Congress—six black members in House |
| **1875–77** | Forty-fourth Congress—six black members in House |
| **1875** | (March 1) Supplementary Civil Rights Act |
| | (November) White Supremacists sweep Mississippi elections |
| **1876** | (March 8) U. S. Senate votes not to seat P. B. S. Pinchback |
| | (July 4) Hamburg, South Carolina riot |
| | (December 14) Wade Hampton inaugurated as governor of South Carolina |
| **1877** | (March 4) Rutherford B. Hayes inaugurated President |

**1877–79**     Forty-fifth Congress—four black members in House
(April 10) Federal troops leave South Carolina
(May 1) Robert Brown Elliott yields office of attorney
general of South Carolina

PART ONE

# BLACK RECONSTRUCTIONISTS LOOK AT THE WORLD

*In this section black Reconstructionists express
their views on a variety of issues of the period. Some of the
persons speaking or writing are political leaders—congressmen
or state officers. Others are minor figures, some of whom give
first-hand accounts of activities of the Ku Klux Klan and other
white vigilante groups. Some of the selections are group opinions expressed in resolutions adopted at conventions and mass
meetings.*

# 1

## Alabama

*On May 3, 1867, soon after Congress (in the Recon-
struction Act of March 2) had provided that blacks should be
registered to vote, a black convention, meeting in Mobile,
adopted the following resolutions.[1]*

Whereas, lately the right of suffrage has been bestowed on our
race, heretofore held in bondage, in order that we may acquire
political knowledge that will insure us protection in our newly
acquired rights,

Whereas, it seems to be the policy of our political oppressors to
use unfair and foul means to prevent our organization and consoli-
dation as a part of the Republican Party in Alabama,

*Resolved,* that we proclaim ourselves a part of the Republican
Party of the United States and of the State of Alabama, and it is in
view of harmony and good understanding not to establish a separate political party that we have assembled.

1. *New York Times,* May 4, 1867.

25

*The meeting also passed a resolution that declared that in the event of the discharge of colored people by their employers for deciding not to become their political tools, they would call for a standing army for protection, and they would make the condition of their people known to Congress and ask for further legislation for their protection.*

# 2

# Arkansas Constitutional Convention of 1868

*In the Arkansas constitutional convention of 1868 there were only eight black delegates out of a total of 66. Nevertheless, the blacks did not hesitate to participate in debate and to answer white delegates who made disparaging remarks about the black race. In the first selection James T. White explains his reasons for voting in favor of the finished constitution.[2]*

## JAMES T. WHITE

*Mr. WHITE* (when his name was called) said: I vote Aye, for this reason. My race having waited with patience, and endured the afflictions of slavery of the most inhuman kind, for two hundred and fifty years, today I find a majority of a Constitutional Convention, that is willing to confer upon me what God intended that I should have. I contend, friends, that the elective franchise is a God-given right, which comes to every man born into the world— be he black or white, green or gray, little or big, it is his right. I desire the elective franchise for another reason. The colored people of these Southern States have cast their lot with the Government, with the great Republican Party that succeeded in putting down the rebellion. They cast their lot with that party, fought with that party, and died with that party; and they have, in consequence, incurred the hatred of the entire Southern people, the Union men excepted. So the ballot is our only means of protection, friends. . . .

Another reason why I shall vote, and why if I had ten thousand votes I would give them all for the Constitution, is, that I see in it a principle that is intended to elevate our families—the principle of schools—of education. That is the only way that these Southern

2. *Debates and Proceedings, Arkansas Constitutional Convention, 1868,* pp. 682–83.

people can be elevated. Were they properly educated they would not to be led, from prejudice, to oppress other men. Were they educated, they would not hate us because we have been slaves. . . .

### WILLIAM H. GREY

*William H. Grey, a free Negro who had come to Arkansas from Washington, D. C. around 1865, was recognized as one of the outstanding orators among black Reconstructionists. At the National Republican Convention of 1872 he delivered one of the opening addresses.*

*In the Arkansas convention a white delegate, Bradley, proposed the inclusion in the constitution of a clause that prohibited performing a marriage ceremony between a white and a person of African descent. Grey replies to this proposal in a speech in which he says something of the sexual mores of the South and the responsibility white men had under slavery for the growth of a racially mixed population.*[3]

Mr. GREY, of Phillips. As far as we are concerned, I have no particular objection to the resolution. But I think that in order to make the law binding, there should be some penalty attached to its violation—kill them, quarter them, or something of that kind. I think, however, the proposed provision is superfluous, for this reason. In the constitutions of the Northern States, where such liberty is extended to men of all classes and colors, such outrages upon society are seldom committed. We hear nothing of them. Among the white people of the North, such provisions are never considered necessary. I cannot see why we should encumber our Constitution with such provisions. I scarcely think, that, with the intelligence and wealth of the white people of the country, they are going to make any overtures to us; and I am pretty sure our condition entirely prevents us from making any such overtures to them. It results, that the provision is superfluous. I know that such provisions have heretofore more or less obtained; but while the contract has been kept on our part, it has not been kept upon the part of our friends; and I propose, if such an enactment is to be inserted in the Constitution, to insist, also, that if any white man

3. *Ibid.,* pp. 362–63.

shall be found cohabiting with a negro woman, the penalty shall be death. [Laughter and applause.] . . .

I desire simply to state that I have no objection to the proposition; but I have so often heard it stated, by some of the grandest minds of America, that such things were utterly impossible, that they were so abhorrent to the feelings, that I thought with Nasby, who says that if you were to put him in a dark room, at twelve o'clock at night, were there the least taint of black blood about a man, he could smell it. I could see, therefore, no necessity for any such provision. In North Carolina, it is declared, by statute, that the issue of negroes, even where one ancestor in each generation, to the fourth inclusive, is white, shall be deemed persons of color. If we are to adopt this proposition, the Legislature will have to pass an act creating a board of scientific physicians, or professors of anatomy, to discover who is a negro. There is the trouble. The purity of blood, of which the gentleman [Mr. Bradley] speaks, has already been somewhat interfered with, in this country. When acts of the Legislature must be passed, making such a distinction as this, to define who is a negro, who is a mulatto, and so on, *ad libitum* and *ad infinitum,* legislation becomes a farce. The insertion of a clause prohibiting negroes and whites from marrying, will not cover the case. You will have to define the point of intermixture of blood which shall constitute a mulatto, and so prevent him or her from intermarrying with the white race; and in the case of an octoroon, or of still further admixture of blood, I take it the distinction will grow very shadowy. The census of the United States shows that forty per cent. of us, already, have crossed the line. It is no fault of ours. No gentleman will lay it to our door. The intermixture has taken place illegitimately. Those gentlemen who so place themselves upon a pedestal of virtue, will not deny that this was wrong. Their own race has thus created the difficulty. I see no way, in the world, of putting an end to the evil by legislation. If you can show where the line can be drawn, I am perfectly willing. But I do not accept the gentleman's idea, that if you raise a fence of legislative prohibition, and a man chooses to crawl under it, it is right enough for him to do so. I propose that we shall stop this crawling under the fence. I propose that if persons desire intermarriage with the other race, it shall be done honorably and aboveboard.

# 3
## Florida

*In the following selections two black Reconstructionists testify before a subcommittee of the joint congressional committee investigating the activities of the Ku Klux Klan. The first witness is Jonathan C. Gibbs, the secretary of state, a native of Pennsylvania, a graduate of Dartmouth College, and an ordained Presbyterian minister. The second witness is Emanuel Fortune, a former slave, who was a member of the 1868 constitutional convention and the lower house of the state legislature. He was forced to leave his home in Jackson County because of fear of the Ku Klux Klan. The men speak of the Klan outrages and the inability of the state government to suppress violence.*[4]

### JONATHAN C. GIBBS

*Question:* Have you information of acts of violence from other counties?

*Answer:* Yes, sir, I have a number of letters in my possession; here is a brief abstract I have made from letters concerning outrages and murders that have been committed in some eight counties; and that is not all. I am certain, to the best of my belief, that I have understated the matter. You will see at the head of this list that I set down one hundred and fifty-three murders in Jackson County. I have stated that publicly in a speech here over a year ago, that that number of murders had taken place in Jackson County. . . .

*Question:* What is the condition of your people generally in this State?

*Answer:* Notwithstanding the difficulties that have occurred, I really believe that the colored people of Florida are better off than they are in any other Southern State; I believe there is more

4. 42 Cong., 2d sess., *The Ku-Klux Klan Conspiracy. Testimony Taken by the Joint Committee to Inquire into the Condition of Affairs in the Late Insurrectionary States: Florida*, pp. 94–95, 165–67, 222–23.

liberty, more personal freedom for them here; that they are doing better, notwithstanding there has been that slaughter. . . .

*Question:* How about schools for your people?

*Answer:* We have at least two schools in this State that are rather above the average of common schools among the freedmen; they are doing in that particular pretty well in view of the circumstances.

*Question:* Where do you get your teachers?

*Answer:* The most of them come from the North.

*Question:* How are they received by the citizens here?

*Answer:* They are badly received. I think we have thirty-one schools open in Leon County; there are a number of white teachers there, and they are ostracised altogether; the people do not recognize them, have nothing to do with them, and talk of them as though they were the offscouring of the earth; that is a common thing. . . .

### EMANUEL FORTUNE

*Question:* When did you leave Jackson County?

*Answer:* In May, 1869.

*Question:* Why did you leave there?

*Answer:* There got to be such a state of lawlessness and outrage that I expected that my life was in danger at all times, and I left on that account; in fact I got, indirectly, information very often that I would be missing some day and no one would know where I was, on account of my being a leading man in politics, and taking a very active part in it. . . .

*Question:* Had there been any men killed in your county before you left?

*Answer:* Yes, sir; several were killed; Dr. Finlayson was killed for one, and Major Purman was shot at the same time; three men were called out of their doors and shot; some were shot through the cracks of the houses, and others as they were going into the houses. I do not remember their names, but there were a great many cases of that kind before I left. . . .

*Question:* Did you hear any expression in reference to your people having a right to vote?

*Answer:* Yes, sir; I have had a great many arguments in reference to that. They would argue very strongly against it. . . .

*Question:* What language would they use?

*Answer:* "The damned republican party has put niggers to rule us and we will not suffer it;" "Intelligence shall rule the country instead of the majority;" and all such as that. They always said that this was a "white man's government. . . ."

*Question:* What is the feeling in respect to your people voting?

*Answer:* They are generally opposed to it; they speak bitterly against it.

*Question:* How do they regard your people getting land and owning it for themselves?

*Answer:* Well, they generally do not interfere with them much, not in that line.

*Question:* Are they ready to sell them land?

*Answer:* No, sir; they will not sell land; we have to purchase land from the Government, or from the State, otherwise we cannot get it. They do not sell our people any land; they have no disposition to do so. . . .

# 4
## Georgia

*On January 10, 1866, more than a year before Congress authorized the registration of black voters, a state convention of freedmen, meeting in Augusta, organized the Georgia Equal Rights Association and adopted resolutions on such matters as natural rights, social equality, land, and compensation for persons held in slavery after Lincoln's Emancipation Proclamation. The resolutions were published in* The Loyal Georgian, *a black newspaper, on January 27, 1866.*

*Whereas,* The colored citizens of the State of Georgia, are here, for the first time in the history of the Government, represented by their delegates in convention assembled, and

*Whereas,* It is a duty which we owe to our common country and the world, to define our position, that all may know what political rights we claim under the Government which has made us free, therefore be it

*Resolved,* That we claim for ourselves the dignity of manhood in common with all other men of whatever race, that we are endowed without any equivocation or evasion of natural rights, but we do not in any respect desire *social* equality beyond the transactions of the ordinary business of life, inasmuch as we deem our own race, equal to all our wants of purely social enjoyment. . . .

*Resolved,* That we discountenance vagrancy and pauperism among our people, and that we will make it our especial business to aid every one to obtain employment and encourage them to earn a competency by honest labor and judicious economy. . . .

*Resolved,* That we deem it the duty of the Government to dispose of any lands it may own to the freed people, at such rates, and upon such terms, as will enable them to pay for them without embarrassment; and thus to secure to themselves and their children permanent homes.

*Resolved,* That all that has been produced by any person occupying lands under the authority of the *United States* belongs to the person or persons producing the same, and no person or persons can legally deprive them of it under the laws of the United States.

*Resolved,* That, whereas, the slaves in certain States and parts of States were declared to be free by Abraham Lincoln, President of the United States, issued on the first day of January, A.D. 1863; therefore, they are justly entitled to receive, and should receive compensation for services rendered by them since that date.

### SAVANNAH BLACKS PROTEST EXPULSION OF LEGISLATORS

*The first legislature elected in Georgia under the 1868 constitution expelled the black members on the grounds that although Negroes had been given the right to vote, the constitution did not expressly give them the right to hold office. A mass meeting of blacks in Savannah protests the expulsion and asks for federal intervention.*[5]

At a mass meeting, of this date, of the republican party, when the entire colored vote of said party in the city of Savannah was represented, called to give expression of opinion in regard to the present status of political affairs in the State of Georgia, and at the same time urge upon the Congress of the United States the absolute necessity of further legislation, in order to secure to every citizen of this State the rights of citizens of the United States, as contemplated under the reconstruction acts of Congress, it was unanimously

*Resolved,* 1st. That the action of the Georgia legislature, in expelling the duly elected colored representatives from that body, was an unjust deprivation of our most sacred rights as citizens, a high-handed outrage on a large political element in this community, in direct contravention of the voice of a majority of the legal voters of the State as expressed at the ballot-box, and contrary to the plain letter and spirit of the reconstruction acts, under

5. 40 Cong., 3d sess., *House of Representatives Miscellaneous Documents, No. 52: Condition of Affairs in Georgia,* pp. 89–90.

which the constitution of Georgia was framed, adopted, and presented for congressional acceptance.

2d. That we cannot hope to have justice done us, to enjoy in security the rights of person or property, freedom of political opinion or thought, or the free exercise of the franchise extended us, as citizens of this State or of the United States, while such fraudulent and unrepublican proceedings of the legislature are permitted to remain valid and of binding force. Further, that the persecutions we have suffered, the barbarities committed in the name of the law, and in defiance of all law, by those in power by virtue of the action of said legislature satisfies us that unless the power of the federal government is brought to bear in our favor our last estate must prove worse than our first, our freedom only another and worse form of slavery. . . .

## HENRY M. TURNER

*Henry M. Turner testifies before a congressional committee about political conditions in Georgia and outrages against blacks.*[6]

*Question:* Please state your residence and occupation?

*Answer:* I reside at Macon, Georgia. I have heretofore been a minister, and am yet. I am now a missionary of the African Methodist Episcopal church, and was lately a member of the Georgia legislature.

*Question:* You are one of the persons expelled from that legislature?

*Answer:* I am.

*Question:* Did you hear Mr. Sims's [another member who was expelled] statement this morning as to the reasons for his expulsion; and if so, are those reasons such as you would give?

*Answer:* Yes, sir; I agree in them. I beg leave, however, to explain the reasons given by him, with a few remarks. The strongest argument that was urged by the democratic party in favor of our expulsion was that no specific rights were given in the constitution allowing the negro to hold office; while we, on the opposite, took the ground that if the negro had no right by virtue of the constitu-

6. *Ibid.,* pp. 10–12.

tion, any rights they had themselves were forfeited by the rebellion, and that Congress gave rights alike to the white man and the black. And we claimed that under the reconstruction acts we had the same rights that white citizens had.

*Question:* Were you a member and the president of the convention of colored people recently held at Macon?

*Answer:* Yes, sir; I was president of that convention.

*Question:* Did that convention represent the negro population of the State pretty extensively?

*Answer:* Very extensively. There were not members from all the counties. The poverty of our people was so great that in some instances two counties joined together and sent one man to represent them both. One hundred and eighty delegates were present from all parts of the State. What is known in Georgia as "the negro belt" was well represented; I mean the middle and southern parts of the State. Several of our delegates had to walk 50 or 60 miles; and one man, I think, walked 105 miles to get to the convention, owing to the fact that neither he nor his constituents were able to pay his fare there by railroad.

*Question:* Was the manner of conducting the presidential election a subject of special discussion in that convention, as to the exercise of the right of voting by the negroes?

*Answer:* Yes, sir. This convention was held just before the presidential election, and there has been no general convention of the colored people of the State held since. A committee was appointed "on murders and outrages," and every man made his report to that committee. A synopsis of the reports was made by the committee, which I would be glad to place in the hands of this committee if they will allow me. . . .

*Question:* Have you information from different parts of the State, since the presidential election, as to the manner in which that election was conducted, and especially as to the exercise of the right of suffrage by the colored people? If so, state that information to the committee.

*Answer:* I have. I may state that in the city of Macon, where I live, I suppose the best moral sentiment prevails among all the citizens, anywhere in Georgia. We have a splendid mayor there. He is a democrat, but is an honest, upright gentleman. . . . We had a fair election in Macon, and the result was that we polled a heavier vote, I believe, than we have heretofore given, amounting to something like 800 republican majority in the city of Macon and county of Bibb. . . . But I must say that in southern Georgia, so far as I have learned from letters received and from persons I have seen coming to Macon with bullets in their legs, bullets in their sides, and bullets in their heads, the evidence is very strong that the election did not pass without great outrages being committed. . . . I would like to say that I have travelled and lectured as much and probably more than any other man in Georgia, . . . and I can say before God, and in view of the judgment, that I have yet the first time to see the first colored man in any meeting—though I have seen them in meetings of from a hundred to four or five thousand—who has ever inaugurated strife with the whites. And I want to say further, that in all these assemblages I have rarely ever seen a drunken black man. They will hurrah and cheer for Grant, or Bullock, or whoever is the candidate, and sing, as the people always do at such meetings; but I have never known them to create a disturbance. . . .

### ATLANTA BLACKS FAVOR CIVIL RIGHTS BILL

*White politicians frequently asserted that blacks did not really want legislation prohibiting segregation and discrimination. A mass meeting of Negroes in Atlanta, on January 26, 1874, protests against such assertions by Senator Alexander H. Stephens, formerly Vice-President of the Confederate States, and in resolutions passed by the Georgia legislature. They praise the speech of Robert Brown Elliott in support of the Sumner Civil Rights Bill.[7]*

Whereas Hon. A. H. Stephens, in his speech before Congress January 5, 1874, said that colored people of the State of Georgia did not desire the passage of the civil-rights bill; and whereas the Georgia Legislature has also adopted resolutions informing the Congress of the United States that the colored people of Georgia do not desire the passage of said civil-rights bill; and whereas the allegations of Mr. Stephens and the Georgia Legislature are without foundation in fact: Therefore,

7. 42 Cong., 2d sess., *Congressional Record*, p. 1312.

*Resolved,* That we, a portion of the colored citizens of Georgia, do most solemnly deny both the speech of A. H. Stephens and said resolutions of the Georgia Legislature, so far as they relate to the colored citizens of this State being adverse to the passage of said civil-rights bill.

*Resolved,* That some arrangement be made by this meeting to deny the fact of the said assertions of Mr. Stephens and the Georgia Legislature.

*Resolved,* That we, the citizens of the city of Atlanta, Georgia, immediately inform the Congress of the United States that we desire a speedy passage of the civil-rights bill, and that we claim it as a right they owe us as members of the republican party, and more particularly as citizens of the United States.

*Resolved,* That we most heartily congratulate and thank Mr. Elliott for his able and pointed speech, January 6, 1874, in the House of Representatives of the United States, in behalf of the passage of the civil-rights bill, and in vindicating the ability and patriotism of the colored citizens of the country.

# 5
## Louisiana

*In April, 1868, in the election of governor, Republican Henry C. Warmoth received 61,152 votes to 43,739 for his Democratic opponent. In the Presidential election in November, the Democratic Seymour–Blair ticket received 88,225 votes, while the Grant–Colfax ticket received only 34,859 votes. This remarkable shift followed a massive campaign of terrorism by which whites sought to intimidate black voters and compel them to vote the Democratic ticket. In parishes where there was little violence the Republican vote was about the same in both elections. But in other parishes where intimidation was rampant the Republican vote all but disappeared.*

*The following testimony by two blacks before a congressional subcommittee throws light on the political attitudes of Louisiana blacks and the methods which were used to compel them to support the Democrats.*

### MUMFORD McCOY

*Mumford McCoy, a blacksmith from St. Helen Parish, was born in North Carolina, where he learned to read and write while still a slave. After Emancipation he became a local leader in Louisiana and helped to organize Republican clubs. He fled to New Orleans after a committee of Democrats visited his shop and threatened to kill him if he did not turn Democratic.[8]*

*Question:* State whether you know of any other cause of the hostility of the whites towards the blacks than that of politics?

*Answer:* Nothing, only politics.

*Question:* Did the planters of that parish refuse to give the

8. 41 Cong., 2d sess., *House of Representatives Miscellaneous Documents, No. 154: Testimony Taken by the Sub-Committee of Elections in Louisiana,* pp. 684–86.

colored men work unless they would join the democratic clubs, or pledge themselves to vote the democratic ticket?

*Answer:* Yes, sir. The democratic party passed resolutions in the court-house in Greensburg, that no white man should give a radical negro employment, that no doctor should give him medical attention, and that no lawyer should defend any case for him. The penalty was great if any white men would give him any employment whatever. . . .

*Question:* Did the colored people in the parish have arms?

*Answer:* Some few had pistols, and some few had shot-guns. They always have had shot-guns since they were free, to hunt with.

*Question:* What proportion of the colored people had guns?

*Answer:* There was about one in ten who had a gun.

*Question:* It was testified before the committee by some democrats from St. Helena Parish that you were a dangerous man, and were attempting to organize militia up there, which scared the white people terribly and made them hostile to the black people, on the ground that they feared an uprising of the black people in that parish. I want you to state fully all about that, whether there ever was an attempt to organize the militia, or whether such a thing was contemplated as an uprising of the colored people of the parish?

*Answer:* It was said that we were going to have the militia all over the State of Louisiana, (that was a rumor which came from New Orleans) to protect the loyal people, so that all could vote. It was considered that if they did not have militia they could not vote on the day of election. The colored people in the parish were anxious for that militia to be raised. . . . The legislature was in session that time, and it was commonly talked of, that there would be a militia law passed by the legislature. If there was such, we wanted to have it in the parish, and we wanted to petition the governor for that purpose. There was nothing else done about it after that. There never was any organization got up.

### SOLOMON WHITE

*Solomon White, a former slave who cannot read or write, is interrogated by members of the Ku Klux Klan subcommittee. His testimony shows that blacks, though ignorant, were not so superstitious as to believe that members of the Klan were ghosts of the dead. He explains his loyalty to the Republicans and his distrust of Democrats.*[9]

*Question:* Do the colored people believe much in these Ku-Klux?

*Answer:* They do not believe that they were dead people. They believed that they were some persons who were doing this; but they all passed off as dead folks. The colored people were afraid to say anything else for fear they might be dead themselves. I would not attempt to do it myself; but, thank God, I am living.

*Question:* Did they really believe that they were living people?

*Answer:* Yes, sir; we believed that they were living people, but we used no means of superstition with them at all.

*Question:* How would the colored people have voted last fall if they had been left to vote as they pleased?

*Answer:* As I believe they would have gone with the radical party, in my neighborhood, so far as I know; for when they first voted, they voted that ticket, and they were as ready and anxious to vote it the last day as the first.

*Question:* Did they know who was running for President?

*Answer:* They spoke something about a good man.

*Question:* Who was he—Mr. Seymour?

*Answer:* No, sir.

*Question:* Who else?

*Answer:* I think it was something like Baum.

*Question:* Was it Blair?

*Answer:* Nary a time Blair.

*Question:* Was it Grant and Colfax?

*Answer:* Mr. Grant was considered in our parish, by the colored folks, as the man who had done a great work.

*Question:* What great work?

*Answer:* He had been in the army and captured Mr. Lee and all his army. He was a great general. . . .

*Question:* Suppose that you colored people had not been killed, or missing, or threatened, and had not been troubled with Ku-Klux, would you not have gone for the democrats?

9. *Ibid.,* pp. 163–65.

*Answer:* If there had been a line made, and if every man had been allowed to take his choice and do as he pleased, I think we would have given a majority for the radical ticket. . . .

*Question:* What good did you expect to come to the colored people if you voted the radical ticket?

*Answer:* I will tell you. From my understanding of the radical ticket they were to give all freedmen free intercourse, to show that he was a free man, and to allow him the privilege of voting. We colored folks thought that if we were allowed to be voters we could, of course, express our own opinions. We did not want to do anything against our masters, but we wished the privilege of voting according to our judgment and knowledge.

*Question:* How did you think you would be benefited if you voted the radical ticket?

*Answer:* My understanding was that the democrats did not want us to be voters, and we wanted to be voters, because that was the highest privilege that could be allowed. They said that a black man had not sense to vote. We wanted to vote the radical ticket, because we believed that the republicans were the men who had given us the strongest constitution, and when our eyes were blind they had torn them wide open.

*Question:* What good did you expect they would do for you after the election?

*Answer:* I do not know that they would have done me one particle of good; but when we were blind they opened our eyes. . . .

*Question:* You say that you would like to have voted for Grant. What office was he running for?

*Answer:* We heard that he was running for equal rights of both parties. If we are free people we want to be free.

*Question:* Is that the office he was running for?

*Answer:* That is what we understood.

*Question:* Who was Colfax?

*Answer:* Mr. Colfax and Mr. Blair, from what we understood, one is a black man, the other is a white man. I have seen their pictures.

*Question:* Which was the white and which the black man?

*Answer:* Mr. Colfax is a black man, and Mr. Blair is a white man, from the pictures. I cannot read. . . .

## P. B. S. PINCHBACK

*P. B. S. Pinchback was one of the most able but contro-*
*versial of the black Reconstructionists. Certainly, his political*
*career was the most complicated. In November, 1872, while*
*he was lieutenant governor, he was elected congressman-at-*
*large. The next month (while he was acting governor during*
*the impeachment of Governor Warmoth), he was elected by*
*the state legislature to a seat in the U. S. Senate. Both elections*
*were contested, and in both cases, after long delays, Pinch-*
*back's claims were denied.*

*In the following selection, Pinchback defends his right to*
*be seated in the House of Representatives. He emphasizes his*
*long record of loyalty to the Republican party and responds*
*to Representative L. Q. Lamar of Mississippi, who has just*
*made a speech citing frauds perpetrated by Louisiana Re-*
*publicans as a reason for rejecting Pinchback's claims.*[10]

Mr. Speaker, I have a clear and unimpeached party record.
From the first day when you clothed me with the right to vote to
the present, I have voted at every election the straight republican
ticket. And what is more than that, I have done that in Louisiana
which few men have done in any portion of this country; I have
shown on several occasions that I held party success above personal
interest. . . . It is always charged that I am not trustworthy, not
reliable, if I dare to complain of the bad faith of some of my
republican associates; and any attempt to expose their perfidy is
held to be a betrayal of the republican party. This class of men
have made all kinds of assaults on me; they have paid public
journals, employed persons at heavy cost to write me down, and
they have published papers in my own State to defame me; and if
I complain, they say that I am trying to break up the republican
party. If I strike a blow in defense of the colored man's interest,
they say I am false to the party. These insidious attacks have lost
their force. I recognize the fact that I am a full-fledged American
citizen, and from this day on I propose to do that which I conceive
to be right, no matter whether it subserves republican or democratic interests. . . .

10. 43 Cong., 1st sess., *Congressional Record, Appendix,* pp. 432–33.

One other very important point was made by the gentleman from Mississippi [Lamar]. He stated that no party can sustain the iniquity, the rascality, the corruption, and the fraud of the southern governments. Now, have the members of this Congress, have the people of this country, ever stopped to consider what was after all the true cause of all the evils that are now the subject of complaint in the South. I know not what is true of the other Southern States, but I can state here, without fear of contradiction, that in the State of Louisiana the responsibility is largely upon the democracy. I can show here by irrefutable facts that in the first election held under the reconstruction acts the democracy of Louisiana, entertaining the insane idea that Seymour and Blair could be elected, treated the reconstruction acts as a nullity, and in many portions of the State instigated and thrust forward the most ignorant colored men that could be found for election to the constitutional convention, with the view of making that convention a farce; and in order to make success certain they put no competing candidates in the field. Of course these men were elected, held seats in the convention, in which they voted with their friends. The constitution was framed, submitted to the people, and ratified. The illiterate men returned home successful statesmen, and from that day to this nearly every man in Louisiana has felt himself every inch a statesman, and from this policy has arisen in a great degree the ignorance that has found its way into the public offices of our State.

But that is not the worst of it. In many instances this policy has been resorted to by white republicans when they have found a colored man with intelligence, cultivation, and sagacity, that they disliked and desired to destroy. The colored people have begun to understand this trick and to appreciate intelligence among their class, and to realize that they are held responsible for bad governments in the South; and I say if you will let them alone and only treat them with fair play, encourage them when they make an effort to do what is right, they will work out their own salvation. When they understand that all bad laws, all peculations, iniquities, frauds, and corruption which are charged upon these governments will at last be laid upon their shoulders and they will be held responsible for the same, in my judgment they will be swift to move in the right direction to rectify any wrongs which may exist by the selection of honest, intelligent, and competent men to administer the affairs of the Government.

# 6
## Mississippi

ROBERT GLEED [11]

*The following testimony is given to the Ku Klux Klan subcommittee by Robert Gleed, a state senator. He describes the activities of white terrorists and explains why perpetrators of such lawlessness are never brought to trial. Gleed strongly supports the Ku Klux Klan Act recently passed by the Mississippi legislature.*

*Question:* Have you known of any schools being interrupted in this county?

*Answer:* The schools in the northern portion, northeastern portion, and northwestern portion of the county have been broken up, and in some places you could not establish schools at all on account of these parties. You could not get teachers to teach them. All the schools in the first district, that is, north of this place, have been broken up, excepting one that was in a thickly colored population or neighborhood; but all the others were broken up that I had knowledge of up there, and some they could not establish on that account. They could not get anybody to teach them up there, for fear of their lives, either white or colored. . . . They were threatening teachers; taking out some people and whipping them, ordering others to go away, and such like things.

*Question:* Do you know, or have you heard of any of these Ku-Klux being arrested and brought to justice and punished?

*Answer:* Not one in this county.

*Question:* What is the trouble in bringing them to justice?

*Answer:* The trouble seems to be that there is sufficient influence in their favor—enough men in the organization, in the first place, to get on the different departments of the judiciary, on the grand jury, and on the petit jury, one place and another—to keep any bill from being brought; and first they terrify parties so they are afraid to report them, and if they should be reported, they get in such

11. 42 Cong., 2d sess., *Ku-Klux Klan Conspiracy: Mississippi*, pp. 478–79.

positions that there can be no bill found against them. . . . They are afraid on account of bodily injury to report a case, and if these parties are reported, they seem to have enough sympathy in the community not to be brought to justice. In this community there has been a great disposition since the passage of what is called the Ku-Klux bill to deny such an organization; but prior to the passage of that bill there was not a child of eight years that would not threaten us in the streets, and all over this county, with these midnight assassins. . . .

*Question:* Was that bill supported by the democrats in your legislature?

*Answer:* They opposed it with all their souls . . . and we supposed they must be accessory to the crime for our oppression and all these assassinations, from the simple fact that if they wanted justice administered, they would not oppose a law suppressing this violence.

*Question:* Do you think the passage of the Ku-Klux bill has had a good effect?

*Answer:* I think if it had not been for the passage of that bill that by this time the reign of terror would have been such that we could not have raised any crop, and there would have been no peace through the eastern portion of Mississippi at least. . . .

*Question:* State what, from your best information, seems to be the purpose of these outrages, if there was any general purpose?

*Answer:* Well, sir, we have thought from their organization and from other indications we have had, that the organization, that is, the purposes of the organization, have been to remand the colored men of the country to as near a position of servitude as possible, and to destroy the republican party if possible; it has been, in other words, political. We believe it had two objects, one was political, and the other was to hold the black man in subjection to the white man, and to have white supremacy in the South; that has been the tendency; and then we have evidence of it from the parties who have sworn and bound themselves together under oaths, that is, in clubs, to do all they can from year to year, and from month to month, as long as they live, to establish white supremacy in Mississippi, and the disfranchisement of the black man. . . .

*Question:* Do the colored people of this county, in the country part of it, feel at liberty to stand up for their rights as against a white, as boldly as a white man does for his rights?

*Answer:* O, no, sir, they can't, nor could not be expected to do so, from their lately being emancipated.

*Question:* Are they regarded as insolent if they do stand up for their rights?

*Answer:* Yes, sir; by the white people.

*Question:* Is it regarded as an offense to be what they call insolent?

*Answer:* Yes, sir; that is regarded as an offense to stand up for our constitutional and equal rights, as equal to other people, that is, white people.

## HIRAM R. REVELS

*Long after his short term in the U. S. Senate, Hiram R. Revels dictated a brief and incomplete sketch of his life to his daughter. The manuscript from which the following excerpt is taken is in the Carter G. Woodson Collection, Manuscript Division, Library of Congress.*

In 1868, in the city of Natchez, Miss., I served as Alderman. All the members of that body, including the mayor, were Republicans. Finding that the management of the affairs in that city could, in my judgement [*sic*] be improved I tried prudently to make that improvement and was successful in so doing. Through the influence chiefly of my much esteemed friend Mayor John R. Lynch I ran for the state senate in Adams county and was overwhelmingly elected as was the entire Republican ticket. At the legislature to which I was elected, an opportunity of electing a republican to the United States Senate, to fill an unexpired term occurred, and the colored members, after consulting together on the subject, agreed to give their influence and votes for one of their own race for that position, as it would in their judgment be a weakening blow against color line prejudice, and they unanimously elected me for their nominee, some of the Democracy favored it because they thought that it would seriously damage the Republican party. When the election was held everything connected with it was quiet and peaceable and I [was] elected by a large majority. My career and work in the senate are too well known to need to be rehearsed here. While there I did all I could for the benefit of my needy and much imposed upon people. But I will only mention here now that I did. That is, I got colored mechanics in the United States Navy Yard for the first time. A delegation of intelligent influential colored mechanics from Baltimore called upon me at Washington and informed me of the object of their visit which was to get employment in the United States Navy Yard to which it had not been possible for any of the most capable and intelligent colored mechanics, to get employment, and I conducted them to the office of the Secretary of War and explained to him the object of their visit to Washington and he (the secretary I forget his name) assured me that as soon as possible they would be appointed and in a comparatively short time they received their appointments. Shortly before my time expired in the senate, Senators Morton of Indiana, and Chandler of Michigan, when I was not aware of it, called President Grant's attention to the fact, that some position should be given to me, to prevent my falling into obscurity when I left the senate, and it would have been done had I not gratefully and respectfully declined the honor upon the ground that I preferred remaining in Mississippi where I could be more beneficial to my race and state from an educational and religious standpoint than I could be in a position out of the state. The then Governor of Mississippi Jas. L. Alcorn, wrote me saying that when my time expired in the senate he advised me to return to Miss, as he had a dignified service for me, and when I returned I learned that the service to which he refered [sic] was the establishing of Alcorn University. The Governor said that he desired to do that thing for the benefit of the colored people of the state of Mississippi and that, that was the most opportune time for doing it by my assistance, that is, I having just returned from the United States senate, would have a large telling influence with both branches of the legislature, so he and I prepared a bill for the establishing of it and I presented it first to the senate and then to the house of Representatives, and it soon became a law and the school was established. As a compliment to me the legislature styled it Revels University but on my earnest solicitation it was named for the Governor Alcorn University.

### JOHN R. LYNCH

*John R. Lynch was speaker of the Mississippi House of Representatives and was three times elected to Congress. In this excerpt from his book,* The Facts of Reconstruction (*New York: Neal Publishing Company, 1913*), *pp. 104–18, he gives his analysis of politics in Mississippi. He stresses the importance of the congressional elections of 1874, in which, for the first time since the Civil War, Democrats gained control of the House of Representatives. This, Lynch feels, gave encouragement to the more recalcitrant elements among Southern Democrats and caused whites to leave the Republican party.*

Since the result of the election [of 1872] was so decisive, and since every branch of the government was then in the hands of the Republicans, further opposition to the Congressional Plan of Reconstruction was for the first time completely abandoned. . . . The colored vote was the important factor which now had to be considered and taken into account. It was conceded that whatever element or faction could secure the favor and win the support of the colored vote would be the dominant and controlling one in the State. . . .

While the colored men held the key to the situation, the white men knew that the colored men had no desire to rule or dominate even the Republican party. All the colored men wanted and demanded was a voice in the government under which they lived, and to the support of which they contributed, and to have a small, but fair, and reasonable proportion of the positions that were at the disposal of the voters of the State and of the administration. . . .

It was the State and Congressional elections of 1874 that proved to be the death of the Republican party at the South. . . . If the State and Congressional elections of 1874 had been a repetition of those of 1872 or if they had resulted in a Republican victory, Republican success in the Presidential election of 1876 would have been a reasonably assured fact. By that time the party at the South would have included in its membership from forty to fifty per cent of the white men of their respective States and as a result thereof it would have been strong enough to stand on its own feet and maintain its own independent existence, regardless of reverses which the parent organization might have sustained in other sections. . . . But after the State and Congressional elections of 1874 the situation was materially changed. The liberal and conservative element of the Democracy was relegated to the rear and the radical element came to the front and assumed charge.

Subsequent to 1872 and prior to 1875 race proscription and social ostracism had been completely abandoned. A Southern white man could become a Republican without being socially ostracized. . . . But after the State and Congressional elections of 1874 there was a complete change of front. The new order of things was then set aside and the abandoned methods of a few years back were revived and readopted. . . . Desertions from the Republican ranks at the South, in consequence thereof, became more rapid than had been the accessions between 1872 and 1875. Thousands who had not taken an open stand, but who were suspected of being inclined to the Republican party, denied that there had ever been any justifiable grounds for such suspicions. . . .

It soon developed that all that was left of the once promising and flourishing Republican party at the South was the true, faithful, loyal, and sincere colored men,—who remained Republican from necessity as well as from choice,—and a few white men, who were Republicans from principle and conviction, and who were willing to incur the odium, run the risks, take the chances, and pay the penalty that every white Republican who had the courage of his convictions must then pay. This was a sad and serious disappointment to the colored men who were just about to realize the hope and expectation of a permanent political combination and union between themselves and the better element of the whites, which would have resulted, in good, honest, capable, and efficient local government and in the establishment and maintenance of peace, goodwill, friendly, cordial, and amicable relations between the two races. But this hope, politically at least, had now been destroyed, and these expectations had been shattered and scattered to the four winds. The outlook for the colored man was dark and anything but encouraging. . . .

# 7
## South Carolina

*In South Carolina, where the ratio of blacks to whites was greater than in any other state, blacks exercised the greatest political power. The South Carolina constitutional convention of 1868 (in which there were 76 Negroes to 48 whites) was the only convention in which blacks were in a majority. At first black leaders hoped and expected to be able to work harmoniously with whites. In the following selections, two local black Reconstructionists, both former slaves, show their desire to conciliate and cooperate with the former master class.*

**BEVERLY NASH**

*Beverly Nash was a member of the 1868 constitutional convention and an influential member of the state legislature. Earlier he attended a freedmen's convention in Washington, D. C. and was in the gallery of the House of Representatives when the Reconstruction Act providing for Negro suffrage was passed. Below is part of a speech (as reported in the* New York Times, *March 23, 1867), which he gives at a meeting in Columbia to celebrate the granting of voting rights.*

[Nash] maintained that being in a majority it would be their [the blacks] own fault if they did not shape their own destiny; but hoped that their exercise of the great power thus put into their hands would be characterized by such moderation and justice as would make neither the National Congress that had given them this right, nor South Carolina, their native land, blush in consequence of their course. While in Washington he had been asked if his people would vote for their former masters; and he had replied that they would vote for loyal and patriotic men, whoever they might be. He believed that his race were as capable of voting properly as were hundreds of the sand hill whites who had been voting all their lives; and that before ninety days they would be exercising that right all over the State. He held that there should be no enmity between the white and the black—that the hatchet should be buried and that cooperation should be the order of the day. He hoped that his race would prove themselves too proud to surrender any of their own rights and too generous to infringe upon the rights of others. He was distinctly in favor of absolutely universal suffrage without distinction of property or education. . . . [He] announced as his confident belief, that in less than twelve months the white man and the negro would be seen walking arm-in-arm to the ballot box, with unity of interests and unity of feeling.

### ROBERT C. DeLARGE

*Robert C. DeLarge, a former slave, was successively a member of the 1868 constitutional convention, the state legislature, and Congress. The* New York Times *(April 9, 1868) reports a speech he makes at a Republican rally, pleading with whites to support the new constitution.*

The thinking white man no less than the colored man is tired of this state of uncertainty and all want a regular government. Whatever tends to injure the white man also injures the colored race, and I appeal to the whites to cooperate with us. The new Constitution asks for the sacrifice of no principle. The true men of my race proved by the Constitution that they desired to oppress no one. I ask—nay I plead—that you whites come forward and bridge over the breach, which should not exist. If the whites would prove that they are willing to extend to others the rights which they desire for themselves, they would be met in the same spirit. If they will come forward even at this late hour, they will find us ready to meet them. . . .

The greatest feat I desire the Republican party to accomplish is to win over the other party. Our most bitter opponents are disposed, I believe, to build up the oppressed race. I trust none of you will be turned aside from voting for the Constitution.

### DEBATES IN THE CONSTITUTIONAL CONVENTION OF 1868

*All of the blacks who later held important political positions took an active part in the debates in the constitutional*

*convention. Although they all agreed upon certain funda-*
*mentals they differed among themselves on some issues.*

### Prohibition of Distinctions Based on Race

*B. F. Randolph (later assassinated by members of the Ku*
*Klux Klan) offers an amendment:*[12]

Mr. B. F. Randolph offered the following amendment: "Distinction on account of race or color in any case whatever shall be
prohibited, and all classes of citizens, irrespective of race and color,
shall enjoy all common, equal and political privileges."

It is, doubtless, the impression of the members of the Convention that the Bill of Rights as it stands, secures perfect political
and legal equality to all the people of South Carolina. It is a fact,
however, that no where is it laid down in the instrument, em-
phatically and definitely, that all the people of the State, irrespective of race and color, shall enjoy equal privileges. . . .

In our Bill of Rights, I want to settle the question forever. . . .
The words proposed as an amendment were not calculated to create
distinction, but to destroy distinction. . . . Here I would say that
all of my radicalism consists in believing one thing, namely, that all
men are created of one blood; that "God created all nations to
dwell upon the earth. . . ."

### Francis L. Cardozo

*Francis L. Cardozo, a graduate of the University of Glas-*
*gow, a Congregational minister, and teacher, speaks in sup-*
*port of the proposed amendment.*[13]

It is a patent fact that, as colored men, we have been cheated
out of our rights for two centuries, and now that we have the
opportunity, I want to fix them in the Constitution in such a way

12. *Proceedings of the Constitutional Convention of South Carolina Held at*
*Charleston, South Carolina, Beginning January 14th and Ending March 17,*
*1868*, pp. 353–54.
13. *Ibid.*, p. 354.

that no lawyer, however cunning or astute, can possibly misinterpret the meaning. If we do not do so, we deserve to be, and will be, cheated again. Nearly all the white inhabitants of the State are ready at any moment to deprive us of these rights, and not a loop-hole should be left that would permit them to do it constitutionally.

### Suffrage

*Most of the black delegates favored universal suffrage, but a few supported a proposal that after a certain date only persons who could read and write would be eligible to vote. Robert Brown Elliott, a lawyer, a future member of Congress, and one of the most brilliant of the black Reconstructionists, speaks against the proposal.*[14]

It is proposed here to restrict the right of suffrage to every person coming of age after the year 1875.

For nearly two hundred and fifty years, we,—I say we, because I believe this to be aimed more directly at the people with whom I am identified than at any other—have been deprived of the rights of education. Even if it had been limited to thirty or forty years, I should still object to this section as it stands. I claim that this Convention has met for the purpose of laying down a basis of universal suffrage. . . . If such a proposition were submitted to the people to decide, and the majority saw fit to change from universal to qualified suffrage, it is their privilege to do so; but it would certainly be wrong for us to attempt to insert any such provision in the Constitution. I trust we will vote down such a provision, by voting for the amendment I have proposed.

*W. J. McKinlay, a teacher, who was free before Emancipation, supports the educational qualification.*[15]

There are some subjects which are extremely unpopular to advocate upon the floor of this Convention. Nevertheless, I think

14. *Ibid.,* p. 826.
15. *Ibid.,* p. 828.

it is but right that a man should divest himself of all prejudices, and look only for the good of the whole country. I have done so, and I have conscientiously come to the conclusion that the amendment I offered should prevail, namely: that all persons coming of age after the year 1878, unless they had certain qualifications and were able to read and write, they should not be allowed to vote. . . . Now, in order to have wise men at the head of our government, it is necessary that the people should be educated and have a full sense of the importance of the ballot. The public schools are to be supported by the public. . . . It is but right if this State establishes a system of free schools, supported by the taxes and money of the people, that it should be demanded by the State that the people should avail themselves of the privileges of those public schools, so as to, at least, be able to read and write. . . .

### Land

*Freedmen regarded the right to own land as one of the greatest blessings of freedom. But little land was available to them. None of the members of the constitutional convention advocated confiscation of the plantations of former rebels. Richard H. Cain proposed that the convention petition Congress to appropriate one million dollars to the Freedmen's Bureau to enable former slaves to purchase land. Cain speaks in favor of his proposal.*[16]

This is a measure of relief to those thousands of freed people who now have no lands of their own. I believe the possession of lands and homesteads is one of the best means by which a people is made industrious, honest and advantageous to the State. I believe it is a fact well known, that over three hundred thousand men, women and children are homeless, landless. The abolition of slavery has thrown these people upon their own resources. How are they to live. . . . As long as people are working on shares and contracts, and at the end of every year are in debt, so long will they and the country suffer. But give them a chance to buy lands, and they become steady, industrious men. . . . I have gone through the country and on every side I was besieged with questions: How are

16. *Ibid.,* pp. 379–81.

we to get homesteads, to get lands? I desire to devise some plan, or adopt some measure by which we can dissipate one of the arguments used against us, that the African race will not work. I do not believe the black man hates work any more than the white man does. Give these men a place to work, and I will guarantee before one year passes, there will be no necessity for the Freedmen's Bureau, or any measure aside from those measures which a people may make in protecting themselves.

But a people without homes become wanderers. If they possess lands they have an interest in the soil, in the State, in its commerce, its agriculture, and in everything pertaining to the wealth and welfare of the State. . . . I do not desire to have a foot of land in this State confiscated. I want every man to stand upon his own character. I want these lands purchased by the government, and the people afforded an opportunity to buy from the government. I believe every man ought to carve out for himself a character and position in this life. I believe every man ought to be made to work by some means or other, and if he does not, he must go down. . . . I propose to let the poor people buy these lands, the government to be paid back in five years time. . . .

### Education

> *Black Reconstructionists had great faith in the beneficial effects of education, and they were unanimous in supporting public schools. But they differed among themselves over whether school attendance should be made compulsory. Robert C. DeLarge objected to a proposal for compulsory education on the grounds that it would be "contrary to the spirit and principles of republicanism" and would also be impossible to enforce. Richard H. Cain regarded the compulsory provisions as "obnoxious" and unnecessary.*
>
> *Alonzo J. Ransier speaks in favor of compulsory education.*[17]

I contend that in proportion to the education of the people so is their progress and civilization. Believing this, I believe that

17. *Ibid.,* pp. 688–89.

the Committee have properly provided for the compulsory education of all the children in this State. . . .

Now I propose to support this section fully, and believe that the more it is considered in all its bearings upon the welfare of our people, the greater will be the desire that every parent shall, by some means, be compelled to educate his children and fit them for the responsibilities of life. . . .

Had there been such a provision as this in the Constitution of South Carolina heretofore, there is no doubt that many of the evils which at present exist would have been avoided, and the people would have been advanced to a higher stage of civilization and morals, and we would not have been called upon to mourn the loss of the flower of the youth of this country.

*Robert Brown Elliott speaks in favor of compulsory education.*[18]

I do not rise to make a speech, but simply and briefly to express the hope that the section as reported by the Committee on Education will be adopted. Some gentlemen have said it is anti-republican. I deny it. It is in conformity with the ideas of republicanism to punish crime. It is republicanism to reward virtue. It is republicanism to educate the people, without discrimination. . . . The only question is whether children shall become educated and enlightened, or remain in ignorance. The question is not white or black united or divided, but whether children shall be sent to school or kept at home. If they are compelled to be educated, there will be no danger of the Union, or a second secession of South Carolina from the Union. The masses will be intelligent, and will become the great strength and bulwark of republicanism. . . .

*Section 11 of Article X of the South Carolina constitution declared that all "public schools, colleges, and universities of this State, supported wholly or in part by the public funds,*

18. *Ibid.,* pp. 694–95.

*shall be free and open to all the children and youths of the State, without regard to race, color or previous condition."*

*A white delegate, B. O. Duncan, spoke strongly in opposition to this section, which he said would require racially mixed schools. The result, he said, would be that public schools would be attended only by colored children—that to attempt to enforce mixed schools would bring "trouble, quarrelling and wrangling into every neighborhood," to the detriment of both white and colored children.*

*Francis L. Cardozo, head of a school in Charleston, answers Duncan. He favors the article, but does not think that it will eliminate all separate schools.*[19]

I think the opinion of the members is so fully established on this subject, that elaborate argument is unnecessary. I shall briefly notice some of the points made by the gentleman. . . .

His first point is, that this provision runs counter to the prejudices of the people. To my mind, it is inconsistent that such an argument should come from a member of the Convention, or from one who favored the reconstruction scheme of Congress. The whole measure of reconstruction is antagonistic to the wishes of the people of the State, and this section is a legitimate portion of that scheme. It secures to every man in this State full political and civil equality, and I hope members will not commit so suicidal an act as to oppose the adoption of this section.

The gentleman from Newberry said he was afraid we were taking a wrong course to remove these prejudices. The most natural method to effect this object would be to allow children, when five or six years of age, to mingle in schools together, and associate generally. Under such training, prejudice must eventually die out; but if we postpone it until they become men and women, prejudice will be so established that no mortal can obliterate it. This, I think, is a sufficient reply to the argument of the gentleman under this head.

We have carefully provided in our report that every one shall be allowed to attend a free school. We have not said there shall be no separate schools. On the contrary, there may be separate schools, and I have no doubt there will be such in most of the districts.

19. *Ibid.,* pp. 900–1.

In Charleston, I am sure such will be the case. The colored pupils in my school would not like to go to a white school. . . .

In sparsely settled country districts, where perhaps there are not more than twenty-five or thirty children, separate schools may be established; but for ten or fifteen white children to demand such a separation, would be absurd; and I hope the Convention will give its assent to no such proposition.

### FRANCIS L. CARDOZO SPEAKS ON THE CORRUPTION ISSUE

*Francis L. Cardozo, state treasurer, was one of the most highly educated black Reconstructionists and a man of unquestionable integrity. In an interview in the* New York Times *(June 22, 1874), he discusses the charges of corruption that Democrats have brought against South Carolina Republicans. He admits there has been corruption but insists Republicans have been taking measures to correct the abuses. He accuses Democrats of using the charges of corruption to justify a possible resort to violence to overthrow the Republican regime, and explains why blacks distrust Democrats.*

Francis L. Cardozo, the present State Treasurer, and one of the most prominent colored leaders in the South, stated that in his opinion the Democrats of the State were eagerly watching and constantly waiting for an opportunity to get control of the State Government. . . . As this was true, it was the duty of Republicans to do everything possible to reform their evils and correct their mistakes. . . . In 1872 the Republicans, at their convention . . . strongly condemned the conduct of those who up to that time had been entrusted with the control of the party and expressed themselves as exceedingly dissatisfied with the enactment and administration of the laws up to that time. Of his personal knowledge Mr. Cardozo knew that there were none more determined or outspoken in their condemnation than the colored men. They felt mortified and humiliated when they saw that they had been deceived by those whom they had entrusted with power. It was then that a platform was presented to the people in which the errors of the party were acknowledged, and retrenchment and reform promised. This effort at better government and all others having the same object in view, were distasteful to the Democracy, who disapproved of them, knowing that if they succeeded the power of the colored voters would be perpetuated. . . . They openly declared that corruption was agreeable to them, as it would hasten the overthrow of the present rulers. The promises of reform made by the Republican Party had not been fulfilled in many instances . . . but it was also undoubted that much improvement had been made within the past two years. . . . [He recounts some of the reforms in state finances that have been adopted in the executive and legislative branches.—Ed.]

The Democrats . . . had observed with growing alarm, that their rivals were redeeming their errors and thus showing sufficient vitality to retrieve their mistakes. They had, therefore, charged the Republicans now in office with commission of wrongs which really had dated back six years, and which the Republicans themselves had admitted to be grave errors, for which party leaders had long ago been punished. It had been said, and Mr. Cardozo believed, with a great deal of truth, that in addition to this attempt to make the Republican party odious in the eyes of the North, the object of the Democrats was to create such sympathy for themselves as would excuse any violent measures they might resort to for the triumph of their party. The Democrats of South Carolina professed to be friendly to the colored men and desirous of securing to them the enjoyment of their civil and political rights. The colored men had no confidence in these professions. Not that they believe there is deliberate purpose to deceive them, but that the Democrats, should they have the power, would assume to be the judges of what their rights were, or should be, and would soon remand the negro to a condition of subjection and dependence that would be substantially slavery. The men who believed that slavery was a divine institution and inaugurated a bloody civil war because this was denied by the merciful people of the North, could not in so short a time have entirely changed their opinions. They still desired the labor of the blacks and would go to any length to control it. The crimes and mistakes committed by the Republicans of South Carolina had been very serious ones, but the Democracy instead of trying to correct, had done everything to augment and increase them. . . . The colored race greatly deplored this unfortunate political antagonism, but they could not and would not take any step toward the establishment of concord and harmony, if concord and harmony meant the sacrifice of their political and civil rights.

## BLACKS PROTEST THE HAMBURG "RIOT"

*The Hamburg "riot" set the stage for the final overthrow of the Republicans in South Carolina. On July 4, 1876, a band of black militia was drilling in a street in Hamburg, a small village inhabited almost entirely by blacks. When two young white men in a buggy demanded the right of way, an altercation followed. Later, whites used this incident as an excuse for demanding that the Hamburg militia be disarmed. When the blacks refused, white "rifle clubs" stormed the armory to which the blacks had retired. In the affray, the blacks were overpowered and disarmed; several were killed.*

*In the following selection, Richard H. Cain addresses an indignation meeting in Charleston. Following his speech, resolutions of protest are adopted. The preamble suggests that the blacks are ready to resort to retaliatory violence, but the resolutions themselves are moderate, simply calling for an appeal to the national government, through legal channels, if the state government does not act.[20]*

There was no reason, he [Cain] said, why the colored people might not join peaceably together in the condemnation of so heinous a crime as the murder of the inoffensive citizens of Hamburg. It is true that they blocked up the streets on the 4th of July; but did not the white soldiers block up the streets of Charleston on the 28th of June? For this offense the colored Militia had been ordered to give up their guns. He wondered if the noble Anglo-Saxon would submit to having their arms taken from them. No! they would not; they knew their rights and the negroes were learning from them rapidly. He desired to be understood as saying that this thing must stop. Every wrong done in this State injures its prosperity, injures its commerce, its agriculture and business, and drives away those people who could best help to build up the common prosperity.

The colored people expected to be law abiding citizens of the State, but they wanted every man who violated the laws of the State to be brought to justice and punishment. . . . The colored men wanted peace, they wanted the right to go where they pleased

20. *New York Times,* July 21, 1876.

and to do what they pleased, so long as they did no wrong. . . . It remains, therefore, for us to unite in denouncing this outrage, and to demand that Gov. Chamberlain shall bring these men to justice and the perpetrators to punishment. . . .

*After Cain's speech the following resolutions were adopted.*

We invoke the consideration of the whole nation, and the powers of the Federal Government, to see to it that the great principles of equal justice before the law, and equal protection under this government, be maintained throughout this nation, so that safety to life and property, and the right to vote as conscience shall dictate to every citizen, shall be forever secured to all throughout the land.

We tell you that it will not do to go too far in this thing. Remember there are 80,000 black men in this State who can bear Winchester rifles, and know how to use them, and that there are 200,000 women who can light a torch and use the knife, and that there are 100,000 boys and girls who have not known the lash of a white master, who have tasted freedom once and forever, and that there is deep determination never, so help their God, to submit to be shot down by lawless regulators for no crimes committed against security and law. There is a point at which forbearance ceases to be a virtue; . . . The negro in this country will not always be docile. . . . The rising generation are as brave and daring as white men. Already that spirit is taking deep root in the minds of thousands who have nothing to lose in the contest, and who would rejoice in the opportunity to sacrifice their lives for their liberty.

*Resolved,* that the massacre of colored citizens at Hamburg, S. C. is unworthy of any civilized community and deserves the censure and condemnation of the civilized world. . . .

*Resolved,* that we call upon the Governor of South Carolina to see to it that the laws of the land be faithfully executed upon all perpetrators of the bloody deed at Hamburg; and be it further

*Resolved,* that in case this one legal demand be not granted, and the protection of our lives, liberty, and property be not to our satisfaction guaranteed and secured by the State Government, then self-preservation, predicated upon the barbarous attitude assumed and being maintained by the whites, warns the colored people to peaceably assemble and petition the National Government through legal channels "for redress of grievances."

# 8

# Black Congressmen Speak

*Selections from speeches made by black members of the U. S. House of Representatives follow.*

## DEMAND PROTECTION OF LOYAL MEN IN THE SOUTH

*Some black Congressmen, aware of the activities of the Ku Klux Klan and other white vigilante groups, opposed the removal of all political disabilities that had been imposed upon former Confederates. Demanding intervention by the federal government to protect loyal men, black and white, they supported such measures as the Enforcement Bill, which gave authority to the president to intervene to suppress violence.*

*In the first selection below, Jefferson Franklin Long of Georgia opposes modification of the test oath. In the next two selections, Robert Brown Elliott speaks in opposition to the removal of the test oath and in favor of the Enforcement Bill.*

### Jefferson Franklin Long[21]

Mr. Speaker the object of the bill before the House is to modify the test-oath. As a citizen of the South, living in Georgia, born and raised in the state, having been there during the war and up to the present time, I know the condition of affairs in that State. Now, sir, we propose here to-day to modify the test-oath, and to give to those men in the rebel States who are disloyal to-day to the Government this favor. We propose, sir, to remove political disabilities from the very men who were the leaders of the Kuklux and who have committed midnight outrages in that State.

What do those men say? Before their disabilities are removed they say, "We will remain quiet until all of our disabilities are removed, and then we shall again take the lead." Why, Mr. Speaker, in my State since emancipation there have been over five hundred loyal men shot down by the disloyal men there, and not one of

---

21. 41 Cong., 3d sess., *Congressional Globe*, pp. 881–82.

those who took part in committing those outrages has ever been brought to justice. Do we, then, really propose here to-day, when the country is not ready for it, when those disloyal people still hate this Government, when loyal men dare not carry the "stars and stripes" through our streets, for if they do they will be turned out of employment, to relieve from political disability the very men who have committed these Kuklux outrages? I think that I am doing my duty to my constituents and my duty to my country when I vote against any such proposition.

Yes, sir; I do mean that murders and outrages are being committed there. I received no longer ago than this morning a letter from a man in my State, a loyal man who was appointed postmaster by the President, stating that he was beaten in the streets a few days ago. I have also received information from the lower part of Georgia that disloyal men went in the midnight disguised and took a loyal man out and shot him; and not one of them has been brought to justice. Loyal men are constantly being cruelly beaten. When we take the men who commit these outrages before judges and juries we find that they are in the hands of the very Kuklux themselves who protect them.

Mr. Speaker, I propose, as a man raised as a slave, my mother a slave before me, and my ancestry slaves as far back as I can trace them, yet holding no animosity to the law-abiding people of my State, and those who are willing to stand by the Government, while I am willing to remove the disabilities of all such who will support the Government, still I propose for one, knowing the condition of things there in Georgia, not to vote for any modification of the test-oath in favor of disloyal men.

### Robert Brown Elliott[22]

Mr. Speaker, the House now has under consideration a bill of vast importance to the people of the section that I have the honor in part to represent. It is a proposition to remove the political disabilities of persons lately engaged in rebellion against the sovereignty of the Government of the United States. I believe, sir, that I have been noted in the State from which I come as one entertaining liberal views upon this very question; but, sir, at a time like this, when I turn my eyes to the South and see the loyal men

22. 42 Cong., 1st sess., *Congressional Globe*, p. 102.

of that section of the country suffering at the hands of the very men whom it is proposed to-day by this Forty-Second Congress of the United States to relieve of their political disabilities, I must here and now enter my solemn protest against any such proposition.

Sir, it is nothing but an attempt to pay a premium for disloyalty and treason at the expense of loyalty. . . .

Sir, I speak not to-day in behalf of the colored loyalists of the South alone. I wish it to be distinctly understood that I represent here a constituency composed of men whose complexions are like those of gentlemen around me as well as men whose complexions are similar to my own. I represent a constituency as loyal as the constituency of any other gentleman upon this floor. Those men appeal to you to-day to do justice to them. They ask you to protect them by legislation, instead of placing them under the heel of those men who have ruled in the South with an iron hand since the reconstruction acts were passed. Sir, I come here backed up by a majority as large probably as that of any gentleman on this floor; I come here representing a Republican district; but unless this Congress will aid those loyal men of the South, unless, instead of passing propositions of this kind, it will turn its attention, and that speedily, to the protection of property and life in the South, the Republican party in this House cannot expect the support of those whom I represent.

### *Elliott speaks in support of the Enforcement Bill.*[23]

I do not wish to be understood as speaking for the colored man alone when I demand instant protection for the loyal men of the South. No, sir, my demand is not so restricted. In South Carolina alone, at the last election, twelve thousand of the working white men in good faith voted the Republican ticket, openly arraying themselves on the side of free government. This class have discovered that the same beneficent system that emancipates the laborer of the one race secures the freedom of the other. They understand that the shackle that bound the arms of the black man threw a deep shadow on the path of the laboring white. The white Republican of the South is also hunted down and murdered or

23. *Ibid.,* p. 465.

scourged for his opinion's sake, and during the past two years more than six hundred loyal men of both races have perished in my State alone.

Yet, sir, it is true that these masked murderers strike chiefly at the black race. And here I say that every southern gentleman should blush with shame at this pitiless and cowardly persecution of the negro. If the former master will yield no obedience to the laws of the land he should at least respect the claims of common gratitude. To him I say that the negro, whom you now term a barbarian, unfit for and incapable of self-government, treated you in the day of your weakness with a forbearance and magnanimity unknown before in the history of a servile population. In the dark days of the war, when your strong men were far to the front, the negro, with no restraint save his own self-control, tilled your fields and kept watch and ward over your otherwise unprotected dwellings. He guarded the person of your wife, the chastity of your daughter, and the helpless infancy of your children. . . .

And how do you requite him now? Be it said to the shame of your boasted chivalry among men of honor in every land, simply because he exercises his privileges as an American freeman, you would drive him into exile with the pitiless lash or doom him to swift murder, seeking your revenge for political power lost by moving at midnight along the path of the assassin!

It is the custom, sir, of Democratic journals to stigmatize the negroes of the South as being in a semi-barbarous condition; but pray tell me, who is the barbarian here, the murderer or his victim? I fling back in the teeth of those who make it this most false and foul aspersion upon the negro of the southern States. . . .

I trust, sir, that this bill will pass quickly, and be quickly enforced. History teaches us that the adequate policy is the best. In one section of the Union crime is stronger than law. Murder, unabashed, stalks abroad in many of the southern States. If you cannot now protect the loyal men of the South, then have the loyal people of this great Republic done and suffered much in vain, and your free Constitution is a mockery and a snare. . . .

## CIVIL RIGHTS

*One of the measures in which black Congressmen were most interested was the Civil Rights Bill, introduced by Sena-*

*tor Charles Sumner of Massachusetts, which was finally
adopted in 1875. The bill prohibited discrimination on account of race in places of public accommodation. The best-
known speech by a black member in support of the bill was
a brilliant constitutional analysis by Robert Brown Elliott.
In the selection below, James T. Rapier of Alabama speaks in
favor of the bill, showing the practical need for it. Having
recently been in Paris (as the U. S. Representative to the
World's Fair) and at the Vienna Exposition, he contrasts the
treatment accorded him in Europe with the treatment he
receives in the United States.*

## James T. Rapier[24]

I must confess it is somewhat embarrassing for a colored man
to urge the passage of this bill, because if he exhibit an earnestness
in the matter and express a desire for its immediate passage,
straightway he is charged with a desire for social equality, as explained by the demagogue and understood by the ignorant white
man. But then it is just as embarrassing for him not to do so, for,
if he remain silent while the struggle is being carried on around,
and for him, he is liable to be charged with a want of interest in
a matter that concerns him more than any one else, which is enough
to make his friends desert his cause. . . .

Let me cite a case. Not many months ago Mr. Cardozo, treasurer
of the State of South Carolina, was on his way home from the West.
His route lay through Atlanta. There he made request for a sleep-
ing-berth. Not only was he refused this, but was denied a seat in a
first-class carriage, and the parties went so far as to threaten to
take his life because he insisted upon his rights as a traveler. He
was compelled, a most elegant and accomplished gentleman, to
take a seat in a dirty smoking-car, along with the traveling rabble,
or else be left, to the detriment of his public duties.

I affirm, without the fear of contradiction, that any white ex-
convict (I care not what may have been his crime, nor whether the
hair on the shaven side of his head has had time to grow out or
not) may start with me to-day to Montgomery, that all the way
down he will be treated as a gentleman, while I will be treated as

24. 43 Cong., 1st sess., *Congressional Record*, pp. 4782–84.

the convict. He will be allowed a berth in a sleeping-car with all its comforts, while I will be forced into a dirty, rough box with the drunkards, apple-sellers, railroad hands, and next to any dead that may be in transit, regardless of how far decomposition may have progressed. . . .

And I state without the fear of being gainsaid, . . . that there is not an inn between Washington and Montgomery, a distance of more than a thousand miles, that will accommodate me to a bed or meal. Now, then, is there a man upon this floor who is so heartless, whose breast is so void of the better feelings, as to say that this brutal custom needs no regulation? I hold that it does and that Congress is the body to regulate it. . . .

Sir, I submit that I am degraded as long as I am denied the public privileges common to other men, and that the members of this House are correspondingly degraded by recognizing my political equality while I occupy such a humiliating position. . . .

Mr. Speaker, nothing short of a complete acknowledgment of my manhood will satisfy me. I have no compromises to make, and shall unwillingly accept any. . . .

Sir, in order that I might know something of the feelings of a freeman, a privilege denied me in the land of my birth, I left home last year and traveled six months in foreign lands, and the moment I put my foot upon the deck of a ship that unfurled a foreign flag from its mast-head, distinctions on account of my color ceased. I am not aware that my presence on board the steamer put her off her course. I believe we made the trip in the usual time. It was in other countries than my own that I was not a stranger, that I could approach a hotel without the fear that the door would be slammed in my face. Sir, I feel this humiliation very keenly; it dwarfs my manhood, and certainly it impairs my usefulness as a citizen. . . .

Mr. Speaker, to call this land the asylum of the oppressed is a misnomer, for upon all sides I am treated as a pariah. I hold that the solution of this whole matter is to enact such laws and prescribe such penalties for their violation as will prevent any person from discriminating against another in public places on account of color. No one asks, no one seeks the passage of a law that will interfere with any one's private affairs. But I do ask the enactment of a law to secure me in the enjoyment of public privileges. . . .

### RICHARD H. CAIN REPLIES TO A WHITE CONGRESSMAN [25]

*In spite of the adoption of the Fourteenth and Fifteenth
Amendments and the presence of black members in Congress, some Democrats continued to assert that this was a
"white man's government." They spoke of Negroes as an inferior race and disparaged their record as soldiers. In the following selection, Richard H. Cain, one of the most effective
orators among the black Reconstructionists, replies to a derogatory speech made by Representative William M. Robbins of
North Carolina.*

I desire to answer a few of the strictures which the gentleman
has been pleased to place upon us. . . .

The gentleman . . . states that the negro race is the world's
stage actor—the comic dancer all over the land; that he laughs
and he dances. Sir, well he may; there are more reasons for his
laughing and dancing now than ever before. [Laughter.] There are
more substantial reasons why he should be happy now than during
all the two hundred years prior to this time. Now he dances as an
African; then he crouched as a slave. [Laughter and applause.]

The gentleman further states that not more than eighteen hundred negroes were killed during the four years of the war. The gentleman forgets some battles; he forgets Vicksburgh; I presume he
does not remember Petersburgh; he does not know anything of
Fort Pillow. He knows nothing about all the great achievements of
the black men while Sherman's army was moving on to victory.
He forgets who entered Charleston first; he forgets who entered
Richmond first; he forgets all this in the blindness of his prejudice
against a race of men who have vindicated themselves so nobly on
the battle-field. But I will grant the gentleman the charity of dwell-
ing no longer on that point. . . .

Sir, I mean no disrespect to the gentleman, but I think the facts
will bear me out in the statement that on every occasion on the
battle-field where the black man met the white man of the South
there was no flinching, no turning back, on the part of the black

25. *Ibid.,* pp. 901–2.

man. He bravely accepted his part in the struggle for liberty or death.

The gentleman says he still looks upon the whites as the superior race. That may be the case in some respects; but, sir, if they educated us they certainly should not find fault with us if we follow out what they have taught, and show ourselves obedient servants.

But, Mr. Speaker, there is another point. The gentleman states that we would make no movement to achieve our liberty. Why, sir, the education which those gentlemen gave the southern slaves was of a peculiar kind. What school-house in all the South was open to the colored race? Point to one. . . .

Examine the laws of the South, and you will find that it was a penal offense for any one to educate the colored people there. Yet these gentlemen come here and upbraid us with our ignorance and our stupidity. Yet you robbed us for two hundred years. During all that time we toiled for you. We have raised your cotton, your rice, your corn. We have attended your wives and your children. We have made wealth for your support and your education, while we were slaves, toiling without pay, without the means of education, and hardly of sustenance. And yet you upbraid us for being ignorant; call us a horde of barbarians!

The gentleman, moreover, states that the reason why they did not educate the colored race was that the colored man was not ready. . . . He says we are not ready for it. How long would it have taken us to get ready under their kind of teaching? How long, O Lord, how long! [Laughter and applause.] How long would it have taken to educate us under the thumb-screw, to educate us with the whip, to educate us with the lash, with instruments of torture, to educate us without a home? How long would it have taken to educate us under their system? We had no wives; we had no children; they belonged to the gentleman and his class. We were homeless, we were friendless, although those stars and stripes hanging over your head, Mr. Speaker, ought to have been our protection. That emblem of the Declaration of Independence, initiated by the fathers of the Republic, that all men are born free and equal, ought to have been our protection. Yet they were to us no stars of hope, and the stripes were only stripes of our condemnation. . . .

The gentleman says that this is a white man's land and government. He says it has been committed to them in a sacred relationship. I ask in all conscience what becomes of our black men and women and children, to the number of five millions; have we no rights? Ought we to have no privileges; ought we not to have the protection of the law? We did not ask any more. The gentleman harps upon the idea of social equality. Well, sir, he has not had so much experience of that as I have had, or as my race have had. We have some objections to social equality ourselves, very grave ones. [Applause.] For even now, though freedom has come, it is a hard matter, a very hard matter, to keep sacredly guarded the precincts of our sacred homes. But I will not dwell upon that. The gentleman knows more about that than I do. [Laughter.]

The gentleman wishes that we should prepare ourselves to go to Africa, or to the West Indies, or somewhere else. I want to enunciate this doctrine upon this floor—you have brought us here, and here we are going to stay. [Applause.] We are not going one foot or one inch from this land. Our mothers and our fathers and our grandfathers and great-grandfathers have died here. Here we have sweated. Here we have toiled. Here we have made this country great and rich by our labor and toil. It is mean in you now to want to drive us away, after having taken all our toil for two hundred years. . . .

The gentleman also talks about the colored people deteriorating. Sir, who tills your lands now? Who plants your corn? Who raises your cotton? I have been in the South during the last ten years. I have traveled over the Southern States, and have seen who did this work. Going along I saw the white men do the smoking, chewing tobacco, riding horses, playing cards, spending money, while the colored men are tilling the soil, and bringing the cotton, rice, and other products to market.

Sir, I do not believe the gentleman from North Carolina wants us to go to Africa; I do not believe it. It was a slip of the tongue; he does not mean that the black people should leave North Carolina; not a bit of it. If they did you would see such an exodus of white people from that State as you never saw before, for they would follow them wherever they might go. [Laughter.]

Sir, we feel that we are part and parcel of this great nation; and as such, as I said before, we propose to stay here and solve this problem of whether the black race and the white race can live together in this country. . . .

# THE WHITE WORLD LOOKS AT THE BLACK RECONSTRUCTIONISTS

# 9

## Southern Whites

*Although some of the following selections express views sympathetic to black Reconstructionists, more express views hostile to them. Some of the speakers or writers are native Southerners; others are Northerners who have moved South. Resolutions of conventions and other expressions of group-opinion are also included.*

### GEORGIA

*A convention of conservatives, meeting in Macon on December 5, 1867, adopted the following resolutions, showing opposition to the Reconstruction Acts and Negro suffrage.[1]*

[The Reconstruction Acts are] wrong in principle, oppressive in action and ruinous to the States of the South . . . [and will lead] directly, if not intentionally, to the supremacy of the negro race in all those States where these laws are now being enforced. . . .

In making this earnest protest against being placed, by force, under *negro domination* we disavow all feeling of resentment toward that unfortunate race. As we are destined to live together, we desire harmony and friendship between them and ourselves; as they are made the dupes of unscrupulous partisans and designing adventurers, we pity them; as they are ignorant, dependent and helpless, it is our purpose to protect them in the enjoyment of all

1. *Appleton's Annual Cyclopedia* (1867), p. 366; *Ibid.* (1868), pp. 309–10.

the rights of person and property to which their freedom entitles
them. . . .

> *The resolutions end with an appeal to the white men of
> Georgia.*

Organize for self-protection and ceaseless opposition to the
direful rule of *negro supremacy* which is sought to be enforced on
us and our children.

### Testimony before a Congressional Committee

> *Dr. S. P. Powell of Augusta, a lawyer and a native of the
> South, describes to a congressional investigating committee
> the intimidation and reprisals against blacks in southern
> Georgia.*[2]

Below Americus there are hardly any white men who maintain the supremacy of the government or of Congress. The colored
people in those counties have been perverted and been compelled
to vote the democratic ticket, even upon the question of the ratification of the constitution. Throughout 10 counties with which I
am perfectly familiar . . . they disapprove of the enfranchisement
of the negro, and have determined to oppose it. The object and
spirit of the people of the State is to put the negro in a semi-serf
condition. They will not consent that he shall occupy any other.
I have travelled extensively in southwestern Georgia and south-
eastern Georgia for the last 12 months, and have been familiar
with the condition of the negro race through all that country.
Their condition is horrible beyond description. I was at Savannah
at the time of the ratification of the constitution. There are large
plantations belonging to the Middletons about five miles from Savannah. The negroes in that county are almost universally republican, and voted for the ratification of the constitution. About the
1st of May the owners of these plantations ordered the colored men

2. 40 Cong., 3d sess., *House of Representatives Miscellaneous Documents,
No. 52: Condition of Affairs in Georgia*, pp. 36–37.

upon them to leave because they voted the republican ticket. They refused to go. They held some imperfect contracts with the owners and the latter called upon the colonel commanding the post, and, as I was informed by an Episcopalian minister, the colonel sent a military force and drove the negroes off these places. They wandered about the country, not knowing what to do. You swore me to tell the truth; I must do it. The negroes, to a large extent, can have no redress from the civil authorities of the State. They have made contracts which have been annulled, and they have come to me in multitudes for redress, as I have been practicing law in Augusta. The cotton is sent off to market and sold by the owners of the plantations, and the laborers are refused their pay. I have tried suits in their behalf in several cases, but have been compelled to quit. The opposition was so strong that a motion was filed against me in court to show cause why I appeared as counsel for these claimants. No language of mine can adequately describe the condition of the negro race in that country; they are so poor; their rights are so disregarded and trampled upon; and there is no redress.

### Alexander St. Clair Abrams

*This selection shows that hostility of white Georgians toward black Reconstructionists could take subtler forms. After the state legislature expelled the black members, Congress required that they be re-admitted. But Alexander St. Clair Abrams, who prepared the manuals of the legislature (which usually included biographical sketches of the members), refused to include biographies of the blacks.*[3]

The reader will perceive that no biographical sketches of the Colored Members appear. Aside from the manifest absurdity it would have been to have written the lives of men who were but yesterday our slaves, and whose past careers, probably, embraced such menial occupations as boot-blacking, shaving, table-waiting and the like, there was, perhaps, another motive prompting the Editor to exclude them from biographical notice. It may have been

3. Quoted in E. Merton Coulter, *Negro Legislators in Georgia During the Reconstruction Period* (Athens, Ga.: Georgia Historical Quarterly, 1968), pp. 179–80. Copyright © 1968 by E. Merton Coulter.

that he felt a secret exultation over the fact that, though Congress could compel him to associate with negroes in a deliberative body, sit beside them in railroad cars, etc., neither Congress, Military Government, a triple Reconstruction, nor even another Amendment to that national patch-work, the United States Constitution, could compel him to publish their biographies in this book. Hence, it may be that, more in assertion of at least one right left, than in any spirit of partisanship, he decided upon keeping them out. Of course, it was necessary to publish their names in the list of members; and this has been done—but this only.

### LOUISIANA

*In June, 1867, a Republican convention, meeting in New Orleans, adopted a platform including the following pledges to recently enfranchised blacks.*[4]

We advocate and will enforce perfect equality under the law to all men, without distinction of race or color; indorse the acts of the Thirty-ninth and Fortieth Congresses; will reconstruct Louisiana upon the Congressional basis, and send to Congress only true and loyal men. Nominations for office to be made only of those who will enforce perfect equality and the right to hold office, irrespective of race or color. We will insist on perfect equality, without distinction of race or color, in the right to vote and enter the jury-box, without any educational or property qualifications being required; also on the right to practise all professions, to buy, sell, travel, and be entertained, and to enter into any and all civil contracts. . . . We will insist on a thorough revision of the laws of Louisiana, that they may guarantee equal justice to black and white alike. . . . As the newly enfranchised citizens constitute a majority of the party, at least one-half of the nominations for elective offices shall be taken from that class, no distinction to be made, whether nominees or appointees were born free or not, provided they are loyal, capable, and honest. The party will always discountenance any attempt on the part of any race or class to assume practical control of any branch of the government to the exclusion of any other race or class.

4. *Appleton's Annual Cyclopedia* (1867), p. 460.

*An editorial in the* New Orleans Commercial Bulletin *(August 29, 1867) declares that "negro domination" is impossible and advises whites that they have it in their power to control the situation by taking the following steps.[5]*

1. By according to the colored race all the political and legal rights to which, as human beings, emancipated from the disabilities of slavery, they are entitled.

2. By elevating the electoral power of the white race by those legitimate agencies which have made it the dominant power elsewhere.

There are legitimate means of maintaining the social standards of the South, and preserving in the hands of the best qualified men the local government of the States and municipalities.

The extension of rights to the freedmen should be frank and cordial. He should vote and be voted for, when his qualifications make him the most eligible candidate. He should never be voted down for his color, nor should any discrimination be made against his labor or his interests. . . . This assurance of course includes the universal education of the freedmen, which will make them better citizens and more productive laborers. This by no means involves the commixture of colors in the same school. . . .

A short synopsis of the comparative strength of the two races in the South will show that there is no danger of negro supremacy, so called, unless the white race is so stubborn and so supine as to surrender all claim to control.

*In the state elections in April, 1868, Louisiana Republican voters, most of whom were recently enfranchised blacks, won a sweeping victory. The committee on resolutions of the state Democratic convention, meeting in September, thus describes the results of the Republican victory.[6]*

Our present State government presents a spectacle calculated to excite no other feelings than those of shame and disgust. The

---

5. Reprinted in the *New York Times* (September 8, 1867).
6. *Appleton's Annual Cyclopedia* (1868), p. 437.

ascendency of the negroes at the ballot-box has enabled them to elect the Lieutenant-Governor and about one-half of the Legislature of their own race, and a large number of reckless and unprincipled adventurers from other States, who have no home or interest here, and are entire strangers to our laws, manners, and customs. These two classes have obtained the absolute control of the State government in all its departments, and have inaugurated a system of profligacy, bribery, and open and shameless corruption that we hope, for the honor of human nature, is without a parallel. . . .

The white people of the State, smarting under a sense of wrong, groaning under an almost intolerable load of taxation, seeing their money daily squandered to enrich needy adventurers, while they are in the same proportion impoverished and ruined, are becoming hourly more restless, discontented, and hopeless of the future.

> *Following the Republican victories in the April elections, white Democrats, through organizations such as the Knights of the White Camelia and the Ku Klux Klan, undertook a campaign of terror and intimidation against blacks in order to carry the state for Seymour, the Democrat in the presidential election in November.*
>
> *The following excerpt from the* Planter's Banner *offers protection to blacks who promise to support the Democrats.*[7]

Blank certificates will be prepared, and every colored person who votes the democratic ticket in November, in St. Mary, will have one of these certificates filled and duly signed, as a proof that he is in harmony with the white people of the country, and it will entitle him always after to be considered the friend of the white man, and entitled to the white man's friendship and protection.

Those colored people who stick to the carpetbaggers till after the election will have the door shut in their faces. They will be too late.

7. *Planter's Banner* (October 17, 1868); quoted in 41 Cong., 2d sess., *House of Representatives Miscellaneous Documents, No. 154: Testimony Taken by the Sub-Committee of Elections in Louisiana,* p. 559.

## MISSISSIPPI

*That some white Mississippians were ready to accept congressional Reconstruction and to recognize the political rights of blacks is shown by the following resolutions, adopted by a meeting of moderate white citizens of Rankin County in 1868.*[8]

*Resolved,* . . . That we recognize the freedom of the colored population of these States as an accomplished fact, and regarding the colored people as citizens, we are in favor of laws that will enforce political equality and rights in the protection of their persons and property.

*Resolved,* . . . That the enfranchisement of the colored man being a part of the policy of reconstruction, which could not be avoided if we would, and which is deemed necessary for the protection of his rights as a freeman, and for the future peace and welfare of the country, we are in favor of a convention, and the adoption of a constitution conforming in its provisions to the requirements of the laws of Congress.

*Resolved,* . . . That we accept and receive the freedom and suffrage of the colored man as fully accomplished, and seeking only the peace and happiness of the people hereafter, we believe it to be the duty of the people of Mississippi and the other southern States to acquiesce in the congressional plan of reconstruction: that all opposition thereto would be utterly futile, and if successful will inevitably entail greater evil than can possibly result from acquiescence.

*Resolved,* . . . That if it were possible to defeat negro suffrage and restore the Union without it, we have reason to believe that the country would have no repose, and we would have nothing to hope for in the future but bitterness and strife, which we sincerely deprecate.

*Resolved,* . . . That the colored people being now free, the interests of both races are identical, and must, in our industrial

8. 40 Cong., 3d sess., *House of Representatives Miscellaneous Documents, No. 53: Conditions of Affairs in Mississippi,* p. 243.

pursuits, and in our political destiny, prosper or suffer alike; it is, therefore, our duty to cultivate friendship and good will one towards the other, and to encourage education and mental and moral improvement among all.

*The following resolutions, part of a platform adopted in 1868 by the Democratic White Men's Party of Mississippi, are probably more representative of white opinion than the above resolutions.[9]*

*Resolved,* That the nefarious design of the republican party in Congress to place the white men of the southern States under the governmental control of their late slaves, and degrade the Caucasian race as the inferiors of the African negro, is a crime against the civilization of the age, which needs only to be mentioned to be scorned by all intelligent minds, and we therefore call upon the people of Mississippi to vindicate alike the superiority of their race over the negro and their political power to maintain constitutional liberty.

*In the following selection, Samuel J. Scord, election commissioner for Copiah County, describes treatment of the newly enfranchised blacks in the referendum for or against the adoption of the 1868 state constitution.[10]*

At Kennedey's Store precinct there was but one vote for the constitution, to wit: "A black man," who, after he had voted, was publicly insulted and threatened with violence if he did not leave the ground and the county. . . .

At Georgetown precinct all passed off quietly; there was no intimidation, except the blacks were told if they voted for the constitution they, the whites, would not furnish them supplies; there was no violence.

9. *Ibid.,* p. 266.
10. *Ibid.,* pp. 173–74.

At Rockport precinct the registrar held the election in a store gallery. Early in the morning, just after the polls were opened, a Mr. Middleton Beasley stood up in the gallery, and cursed and abused any man who would support the constitution, threatened the blacks, and said he was ready to sink any man white or black in the bottom of hell who would offer to vote the republican ticket. A Mr. S. D. Ramsey made a speech within three feet of the registrar, in which he told the blacks that he was taking their names down, and all who voted the republican ticket would be watched and remembered, and would be compelled to leave the country; that they would be turned out, and ought to be turned out with their families to starve. . . . There was not a man, white or black, up to the time I left the ground, that voted or dared to vote for the constitution or the republican ticket. . . .

At Hazlehurst precinct there were very many persons present from all parts of the county; there were some few United States troops with us, but the number was so small they could hardly do any good only near the place of voting or the boxes. There were some 200 republican blacks formed in procession near the residence of Mr. Harvey, for the purpose of marching to the polls; they were proceeding with banners, pictures, and quite a number of small United States flags, without music or any yelling or noise of any kind whatever; they had not got 50 yards before they were met by a mob, their banners, pictures, and flags taken from them and broken and torn up, and then brick-batted and chased to the private residence of Mr. Harvey. I learn that some of the men composing the mob were deputy sheriffs of the county, not suppressing the riot, as they were in duty bound to do under the law, but encouraging the mob by their shouts and yells. It was apparent to me that the republican candidates were not permitted to go out electioneering as the democratic candidates were, but were subject, if they left the presence of the troops, to insults and abuse. There were many of the republican blacks that were in the procession who were frightened out of town and did not vote at all. I learn there were very many more who left without voting, and some were even followed out of town and flew to the bushes, or took shelter in private houses for protection. I cannot undertake to cite to you particular outrages committed here and elsewhere on persons, it has been so general; I deem it unnecessary, however; if you wish, I can establish what I have charged by the written affidavits of both white and black men, and can furnish you, should you want it, names of persons witnessing the charges above.


*Joshua S. Morris, Republican attorney general of Mississippi, a lawyer, and a native Southerner, testifies before a subcommittee of the Ku Klux Klan investigating committee. He cites the beneficial results of the acquisition of legal and constitutional rights by former slaves.*[11]


The right to vote, the various measures which have been passed by Congress for the protection of the colored people, and the constitutional amendments, have raised the condition of those people vastly in every way. They behave better, work better; and I believe they are almost universally well disposed toward the white people, particularly their old masters and families, to whom they have no dislike except as to their politics.

*Question:* You say they are rapidly improving and becoming more fit for the exercise of suffrage?

*Answer:* Yes, sir; they are more moral, more industrious, better citizens in every way than they were before.

*Question:* Are they, as a general thing, ambitious to learn and become intelligent?

*Answer:* Yes, sir. The children go to school, as do also many of the adults, and they learn rapidly. I have seen colored children learn as rapidly as I ever saw white children learn. Going along the street I have seen little fellows of an age at which you would hardly expect white children to read, spelling the signs on the doors; and I have seen them reading books and newspapers. I have occasionally visited their schools and heard them recite, and they show a great degree of improvement. I believe that the people of Mississippi generally are improving now. I think that, notwithstanding they have had a great deal of misfortune, loss, and ruin throughout the State, resulting from the war, they are now substantially in a better condition than they were before the war. They have not so much money, but they are more disposed to work and

11. 42 Cong., 2d sess., *Ku-Klux Klan Conspiracy: Mississippi,* p. 306.

get along; and I think there is a better state of feeling toward the freedmen. The old politicians, though, will never get over it— never in the world.

*Question:* They will never believe in the new order of things?

*Answer:* Never. They have been turned out of office; many of them have no prospect of getting into office again unless something almost equivalent to a revolution should occur, and they are very bitter. I do not mean all of them; I mean a great many of them. Some of them are very kind and reasonable about the matter, and do not manifest much concern about obtaining office or about politics—never say anything about it; but I think a majority of that class are most intensely bitter in their feelings against the Government.

### SOUTH CAROLINA

*That South Carolina whites were determined to maintain white supremacy and were unreconciled to participation by the blacks in politics and government is shown by the following address, adopted by a state Democratic convention, meeting April 2 and 3, 1868.*[12]

### Address to the Colored People of South Carolina

The convention of the democratic party of South Carolina feels it a high and bounden duty to speak to you candidly and earnestly, and with no further apology than that our interests are to a certain extent identical.

You have been suddenly put in position to exercise certain powers, the abuse of which may result disastrously to you and to us. *It is impossible that your present power can endure, whether you use it for good or ill.* The white race already outnumbers you in the South. Disease has made the mortality among you twice what it is among the whites, and the rate is daily increasing. Emigration has carried off thousands of your color to distant States, while it already begins to fill their places with whites from Europe. Let not your pride, nor yet your pretended friends, flatter you into

12. 42 Cong., 2d sess., *Ku-Klux Klan Conspiracy: South Carolina*, pp. 1253–54.

the belief that you ever can, or ever will, for any length of time, govern the white men of the South. The world has never seen such a spectacle, and its whole history, and especially the history of your race, gives no ground for the anticipation. Perhaps, however, you expect to attain power by the aid of the radical party at the North. The Almighty, in His wisdom, (perhaps to prevent the amalgamation of the separate races which He created and marked,) has implanted in every human breast a sentiment called the *prejudice of race;* and when this feeling is once aroused, it is one of the strongest and most universal passions of our natures. When your race was among us as slaves, this sentiment slumbered, and only a compassion for you influenced every honest heart—those among your masters—to treat you kindly; those who believed you wronged, to desire to set you free. When you were set free, compassion ceased to exist. When undue power was given you by the radical party, (from motives which all men appreciated and despised,) prejudice of race sprang up. . . .

To repeat, then, as we began: Your present power must surely and soon pass from you. Nothing that it builds will stand, and nothing will remain of it but the prejudices it may create. It is, therefore, a most dangerous tool that you are handling. Your leaders, both white and black, are using your votes for nothing but their individual gain. . . .

### A Black Political Rally Described by a Native White

> *Testifying before the subcommittee investigating the Ku Klux Klan, Alexander P. Wylie of Yorkville, a physician who was a Unionist during the Civil War, describes a political meeting held by blacks and gives an account of a speech he delivered to them. Wylie says that blacks have become more violent and unmanageable since being given the right to vote and bear arms.*[13]

The negroes had a meeting at Landsford. . . . Well they [the speakers] were composed largely of the clergy. . . . I was passing there. . . . They were having a barbecue and I never in my life heard such incendiary speeches dragged into a meeting, and

13. *Ibid.,* pp. 1439–40.

earth would ring whenever they uttered those sentiments. It was, "The negroes get together, right or wrong; the negroes must have land or blood." After they had gone through and there seemed to be no dissenting voice, they urged the whites to speak. As I said, there were very few whites there. Some of them called me. . . . I got up and told them, "You must not interrupt me now if I speak, . . ."

I got up and gave them the history of what they had done. I said to them you should be satisfied with your condition. You have done nothing in the advancement of civilization in this world except what has been forced on you through slavery of white men, but you ought not to grumble; the Almighty made you so. I do not think you are as smart as we are, but you have an opportunity in this country to save yourselves, and, though you never before did it, and ultimately you must become a great people, if you do not get drunk on liberty, as the whites, and even be greater and become the leader of the column. I went on and gave them the history of San Domingo. . . . They did not interrupt me much. . . . They interrupted me some, and said, "You wish to make us out brutes." I told them no, I did not. He [sic] said they never had had the chance of the white people. I said why, in taking the chances, did not Africa take the chances and be civilized? It was as old a country as any in the world, but you Africans have never done anything but what has been forced upon you, and it is my duty to tell you the truth, that you are running wild here. It is your duty, if you wish to prosper, to affiliate with the respectable white people. You are a small number of people here, only three or four millions, and there are on this continent forty millions of whites. This party division may last for a while, but in course of time it will drop through, and the lines of the State will be overrun, and they will play the same game on you that you are playing on us.

## Opposition to Black Militia

*White Southerners regarded the organizing of black militia companies, supplying former slaves with arms, as an insult and as one of the chief threats to white supremacy. In the following selections, white South Carolinians show their resentment and express the opinion that the organization of the militia units was politically motivated.*

*Richard B. Carpenter, a judge and a leader of the Reform Party, testifies before the subcommittee of the Ku Klux Klan committee.*[14]

Another cause of discontent was the organization and arming of the militia of the State, and the furnishing them with ammunition. The militia were confined to colored people. Numerous applications were made by white companies to be received into the state militia, but they were all rejected. Some twenty thousand colored people in different parts of the State were armed with Winchester and Springfield and other rifles, and near the time of the election ammunition was distributed to them, as if upon the eve of battle. They were sometimes very offensive and did a great deal of mischief. It was very offensive to the white people that these colored people should be armed, and sometimes depredations were committed by them; that was a serious cause of discontent. . . .

*Question:* What I am coming to is this. . . . Will you state to the committee what effect it had upon the people and their sense of security when the governor armed them [Negroes] as State militia, and refused to arm white people in the same way?

*Answer:* Well, sir, the people felt they had no security at all; that they might be attacked at any time. I do not think myself that this militia was ever organized for the purpose of any war on the white people. It was organized to carry the election through the colored vote, to intimidate and overawe the colored people. I do not think they ever intended to have any fight with the white people, but, of course, the white people felt very anxious upon the subject, hearing companies of colored men drilling and training every night in each village of two or three thousand inhabitants, and the people were perfectly unprotected. In the time of election there was a great deal of whisky about, for the colored man is not very much unlike his white brother in that respect; he is very fond of whisky. And it is very astonishing to me the paucity of casualties and crimes that occurred in consequence of it. They seemed to content themselves with carrying out the ideas of the party. On the day of election they were parading, and then, not where there

14. *Ibid.*, pp. 227–28, 240–41.

were many white people, but in the dense colored districts they overawed and drove off everybody that was obnoxious to them. I think that was the original purpose of the militia, for certainly Governor Scott was in the army too long to suppose that this militia would be effective in any contest with the white people of South Carolina. . . .

*Question:* Was there anything in the militia law that prevented the organization of white men as militia, and their being armed as such?

*Answer:* No, sir. Under the law the governor had the right to receive any organization for militia purposes; the governor had to receive them. . . . When a white company was organized and offered to the governor he invariably refused it, until very lately.

> *C. H. Suber, a lawyer of Newberry County testifies. He is questioned by Mr. Beck and Mr. Blair, members of the committee.*[15]

By Mr. Beck:

*Question:* So that the only armed organizations you have had in the county of Newberry have been colored?

*Answer:* Yes, sir.

*Question:* You think you had six companies of them?

*Answer:* I think there were six in the county; there were three at the court-house.

*Question:* What was their assumed object in attending political gatherings in an organized military form, with arms in their hands?

*Answer:* I suppose it was to please and to dazzle their own people, and at the same time to resist any disturbance that might occur, if any should come in their way; I cannot imagine what else they went armed for. They had their cartridges and their bayonets, and I suppose it was for that; I do not know what it was for.

By Mr. Blair:

*Question:* Did they attempt in any way to intimidate the whites?

*Answer:* They marched through our streets frequently, and shoved everybody off the sidewalks who came in contact with them.

15. *Ibid.,* pp. 146–47.

Indeed, nobody cared to go into the streets when they were parading; it was unsafe for ladies to walk the streets when they were out. Their celebrations generally occurred in a grove not far from the town; and they generally closed their celebrations by marching into the court-house square and occupying the court-house porch or steps, from which harangues were delivered to them. The companies would be formed in front of the court-house, and they would occupy the whole square; the square is rather small.

*Question:* What was the character of the harangues delivered to them?

*Answer:* I was compelled to hear them, because my office was within hearing and I could not do otherwise than hear them. I have heard some of a very incendiary character, the tenor of which was to persuade those colored people that the white men were their enemies; to look upon them as their former masters and as tyrants, and not to trust them in anything. They would dwell with peculiar unction upon the miseries of their former servitude; they would talk to them about the lashes that had been put on their backs by their masters, and the manacles on their hands that had been taken off by their friends, the republicans. They would tell them that they must not trust their former masters, for they were only seeking to get into a position where they could reenslave them. All sorts of appeals were made to their passions, and everything was said to inflame them against the white people.

# 10

## Members of Congress Look at Black Reconstructionists

*This section is taken from the debates in the U. S. Senate and House of Representatives. Members of Congress express their views on black colleagues, the Negro race, and the role of blacks in Reconstruction.*

### MEMBERS DEBATE THE SEATING OF THE FIRST BLACK SENATOR

*Hiram R. Revels was elected by the Mississippi legislature to fill the unexpired term of Jefferson Davis. When he presented his credentials, the Senate debated for three days over his eligibility before voting to seat him. The principal objection alleged by opponents was that under the dicta of the Dred Scott opinion Revels did not meet the constitutional requirement of nine years United States citizenship. Other Senators vigorously defended Revels and his right to be seated.*

*Senator Garrett Davis of Kentucky speaks in opposition to seating "this man Revels."* [16]

There are men who will vote for the admission of Revels here that would quail before that responsibility if they were in the House of Representatives because they would know that they had to confront their master. Such is the insidious and stealthy progress of the Radical party, and especially in relation to negro suffrage and negro equality. . . .

And now, in conformity with this policy, this insidious policy, this man Revels is to be brought to the Senate, and a negro is to be admitted as a Senator before one is admitted to the other House.

Mr. President, this is certainly a morbid state of affairs. Never before in the history of this government has a colored man been elected to the Senate of the United States. To-day for the first time one presents himself and asks admission to a seat in it. How does

16. 41 Cong., 2d sess., *Congressional Globe*, p. 1510.

he get here? Did he come here by the free voices by the spontaneous choice of the free people of Mississippi? No, sir; no. The sword of a military dictator has opened the way for his easy march to the Senate of the United States. . . .

Now, sir, I say that Revels is not a citizen. . . . He is not a citizen by the decision of nine of the judges of the United States in the Dred Scott case. . . .

*Senator James Nye of Nevada replies to Davis of Kentucky.*[17]

Sir, I never expected to hear read in the Senate of the United States, or in any court of justice, where authority was looked for, the Dred Scott decision. Its author and the decision itself have sunk so deep into oblivion that the bubbles will never rise from them. . . .

No, sir, the days for judicial bulwarks have passed, the majority of the people is seen going along in its strength until one of the despised race and color stands now at your bar, not only clothed in the habiliments of a citizen, but clothed with the official power as a Senator on this floor.

Sir, it seems to me that this is the crowning glory of a long series of measures. It seems to me that this is the day long looked for, when we put into practical effect the theory that has existed as old as man. We say that all men are brothers; whatever their color all are subject to the same law, and all are eligible to fill any place within the gift of the people.

Is the honorable Senator from Kentucky afraid to enter in the race for future glory with these colored men? . . .

*Senator Davis replies to Nye.*[18]

The honorable Senator . . . has twitted me with my prejudice against color. . . . I would put it to the Senator's candor, if I

17. *Ibid.,* pp. 1514–15.
18. *Ibid.,* p. 1515.

were disposed to do, but I am not, whether if he knew that every enfranchised negro would vote against him and his party he would be so anxious in support of their rights as he is. I will not ask him to answer such a question; but I will say that the honorable Senator and every Radical Senator in this body is as much prejudiced against that color as I am. Now, I have not seen that the honorable Senator has ever waited upon some colored Dinah to a ball. I have not seen that he has ever extended any of his gallantries to them. I have not known a solitary Senator who is so clamorous in favor of the rights of the negro and the equality of the races, that he has made sedulous court to any one fair black swan, and offered to take her to the altar of Hymen. [Laughter.] . . .

*In the continuing debate over the seating of Revels, Senator George Williams of Oregon insists that the Dred Scott opinion does not apply to Revels because Revels apparently has a preponderance of white blood, and there is no evidence that his ancestors had been slaves. Senator Simon Cameron of Pennsylvania replies:[19]*

I do not think I should have attempted to say a word if the honorable Senator from Oregon had not got up to make an argument that this man has more of white than of black blood in his veins. What do I care which preponderates? He is man, and his race, when the country was in peril, came to the rescue. . . .

I admit that it somewhat shocks my old prejudices, as it probably does the prejudices of many more here, that one of the despised race should come here to be my equal; but I look upon it as the act of God. . . .

### CONGRESSMEN DEBATE THE SUMNER CIVIL RIGHTS BILL

*Following Robert Brown Elliott's speech, on January 6, 1874, in support of the Sumner Civil Rights Bill, Representative Benjamin Butler of Massachusetts speaks.[20]*

19. *Ibid.,* p. 1544.
20. 43 Cong., 1st sess., *Congressional Record,* pp. 455–58.

I should have considered more at length the constitutional argument, were it not for the exhaustive presentation by the gentleman from South Carolina [Elliott] of the law and the only law quoted against us in this case which has been cited, to wit, the Slaughter House Cases. He, with the true instinct of freedom, with a grasp of mind that shows him to be the peer of any man on this floor, be he who he may, has given the full strength and full power of that decision of the Supreme Court. . . .

Now, Mr. Speaker these men [blacks] have fought for their country; one of their representatives has spoken, as few can speak on this floor, for his race; they have shown themselves our equals in battle; as citizens they are kind, quiet, temperate, laborious; they have shown that they know how to exercise the right of suffrage which we have given to them, for they always vote right; they vote the republican ticket, and all the powers of death and hell cannot persuade them to do otherwise. [Laughter.] They show that they knew better than their masters did, for they always know how to be loyal. They have industry, they have temperance, they have all the good qualities of citizens, they have bravery, they have culture, they have power, they have eloquence. And who shall say that they shall not have what the Constitution gives them—equal rights? [Continued applause.]

*Southern Democrats disagree strongly with Butler's view of black Reconstructionists and the desirability of the Civil Rights Bill. Representative John Harris of Virginia speaks against the bill and disparages blacks. Alonzo Ransier of South Carolina attempts to answer him.*[21]

Having discussed the power of Congress to pass this bill, I now ask the attention of the House to its effect as a practical measure, if it shall unfortunately become a law. It is based upon the purpose, the theory, of the absolute equality of the races. It seeks to enforce by law a doctrine which is not accepted by the minds nor received in the hearts of the people of the United States—that the negro in all things is the equal of the white man. And I say

21. *Ibid.*, pp. 376–77.

there is not one gentleman upon this floor who can honestly say he really believes that the colored man is created his equal.

*Mr. Ransier:* I can.

*Mr. Harris, of Virginia:* Of course you can; but I am speaking to the white men of the House; and, Mr. Speaker, I do not wish to be interrupted again by him.

Mr. Speaker, I assert no new theory, unknown to the American mind or unasserted by American statesmen, North or South, when I declare that there is no real equality between the African and Caucasian races. . . .

Now, sir, what does this bill propose? It proposes to put all upon an equality, and to force it upon the people of the country whether they are willing or not. . . .

Now, Mr. Speaker, I know the objection that will occur to the mind of every gentleman on the other side of the House, and of every one here who differs from me on this question. They will say this is prejudice—unjust prejudice. Admit that it is prejudice, yet the fact exists, and you, as members of Congress and legislators, are bound to respect that prejudice. It was born in the children of the South; born in our ancestors, and born in your ancestors in Massachusetts—that the colored man was inferior to the white.

*Mr. Ransier:* I deny that.

*Mr. Harris, of Virginia:* I do not allow you to interrupt me. Sit down; I am talking to white men; I am talking to gentlemen. . . . I did not desire to be interrupted, and the person who interrupted me was out of order in doing so. . . .

*The Speaker* pro tempore: The gentleman will proceed.

*Mr. Harris, of Virginia:* Yes, sir. I thank you, and will do so. I say, sir, that prejudice may exist, but it is a natural prejudice, a prejudice that God himself placed in the hearts of southern children and the southern people, and it becomes us to consider that prejudice in our action here. . . .

*Representative Robert Vance of North Carolina speaks against the Civil Rights Bill, saying it protects "social rights" and raises false hopes among blacks. Joseph H. Rainey of South Carolina challenges him.*[22]

22. *Ibid.*, pp. 554–56.

Why, then, do we oppose the civil-rights bill? That is the question; and speaking as I do, and feeling as I speak, without prejudice, . . . what is the real objection to the bill known as the civil-rights bill. I think gentlemen of the House will bear me out when I say the title of the bill we had before us ought to be changed, and made to read thus: "A bill to protect the colored people in their social rights." That is the way it should read.

Now, Mr. Speaker the distinguished gentleman from Massachusetts [Mr. Butler] laid down the law, and it has not been controverted, that all men are entitled under the law to the right to go to a hotel, to ride in a public railway carriage, to interment, and to be taught in the public schools sustained by moneys raised by taxation. . . . There is no railway car in all the South which the colored man cannot ride in. That is his civil right. This bill proposes that he should have the opportunity or the right to go into a first-class car and sit with white gentlemen and white ladies. I submit if that is not a social right. There is a distinction between the two. Now, there is not a hotel in the South where the colored man cannot get entertainment such as food and lodgings. That is his civil right. The bill of the committee provides that there shall be no distinction. Even if he is allowed to go into the dining-room, and is placed at a separate table because of his color, it will be a violation of this law. Placing him, therefore, at the same table with the whites is a social right. . . .

There is another objection to this bill. It begets hopes and raises an ambition in the minds of the colored man that can never be realized. It is true, sir, that we can find some ten or twelve members of Congress here from densely-populated regions of the South where the colored race is dominant. But how is it in other States? Where is the colored man from Massachusetts? Is he here? Where is even Fred Douglass, who is acknowledged to be a man of ability? Is he here? No, sir; he has not found his way into this House. This bill, therefore, as I have said, begets in the minds of these people hopes and an ambition that can never be realized; and in that view of the case it is unfortunate for them. . . .

Another view of this question, Mr. Speaker, is this: that by placing the colored race and the white race continually together, by throwing them into social contact, the result will be more or less that the distinction between them will be broken down, and that miscegenation and an admixture of the races will follow. Sir, it must necessarily follow on such close intercommunication. I presume that no man will stand upon this floor and say that it is best for all the races of men on the face of the earth to become one by amalgamation. . . .

Sir, it is absurd for gentlemen to talk about the equality of the races. But let us give to the colored man the opportunity of improvement; let us give him an education. I for one will vote cheerfully and gladly for the appropriation of a portion of the proceeds of the splendid domain of this country for the education of the colored race; but I think it ought to be done in separate schools. Sir, we have already given him the opportunity to be educated; we have allowed him to hold office; we have seen and heard colored men on this floor; they are here now. . . .

*Mr. Rainey:* Before the gentleman sits down I would like to ask him a question.

*Mr. Vance:* Certainly.

*Mr. Rainey:* The gentleman has just said that if he was a colored man he would not ask Congress to pass the civil-rights bill, which has for its object the removal of the disabilities imposed upon us by prejudice. I ask him what he thinks of those Southerners who ask Congress to remove from them their political disabilities on account of their action toward this Government?

*Mr. Vance:* I might have expected something of that kind. I find that everywhere men are disposed to bring up the horrid skeleton of the war. Wherever a southern man goes he is almost sure to be confronted with the fact that he was a rebel, if you please; yes, sir, a rebel. I say it was right for the Congress of the United States to remove the disabilities of those men, and place them on an equality with others before the law. We have now been placed equal before the law. The colored man is placed equal before the law. I ask gentlemen why it is that the war is always flaunted in our faces?

## MINORITY REPORT OF THE KU KLUX KLAN COMMITTEE

*Below is a portion of the minority report, signed by the Democratic members of the joint committee of Congress, to investigate the Ku Klux Klan outrages in the South. Minimizing voluminous evidence of violence and lawlessness com-*

*mitted by whites, the report concentrates on alleged deficien-*
*cies of Republican governments in the South and alleged*
*attempts by carpetbaggers and scalawags to exploit black*
*voters. It paints a dire picture of the disastrous results of Ne-*
*gro suffrage and political activity, particularly in South Caro-*
*lina. The point of view and the rhetoric of the minority report*
*significantly influenced later historical writing on Reconstruc-*
*tion.*[23]

The antagonism, therefore, which exists between these two
classes [white and black] of the population of South Carolina does
not spring from any political cause, in the ordinary sense of the
term, but it grows out of that instinctive and irrepressible repugnance to compulsory affiliation with another race, planted by the
God of nature in the breast of the white man, perhaps more
strongly manifested in the uneducated portion of a people, and
aggravated and intensified by the fact that the negro has been
placed as a *ruler* over him. This is not the place to discuss negro
suffrage or negro equality, even in a government or State where
the negro is in a controlling majority; but we cannot refrain from
declaring right here that no fair-minded man, we care not what
may be his prejudices or his party ties, can go down to South
Carolina and see the practical workings of the system there without
being driven to the admission that the policy which has made a
San Domingo of one of the States of this Union is one of the
most terrible blunders ever committed, one of the most reckless
and unwise political movements ever inaugurated in a government
of fixed laws and constitutions.

As we have just remarked, we do not propose to discuss at large
the question of negro government in these pages; but we feel that
it would be a dereliction of duty on our part, if, after what we
have witnessed in South Carolina, we did not admonish the American people that the present condition of things in the South cannot last. It was an oft-quoted political apothegm, long prior to the
war, that no government could exist "half slave and half free." The
paraphrase of that proposition is equally true, that no government
can long exist "half black and half white." If the republican party,

23. 42 Cong., 2d sess., *Ku-Klux Klan Conspiracy,* Vol. I, pp. 515–17; 524,
526–27, 558–59, 579, 583–84.

or its all-powerful leaders in the North, cannot see this, if they are so absorbed in the idea of this newly discovered political divinity in the negro, that they cannot comprehend its social repugnance or its political dangers; or, knowing it, have the wanton, wicked, and criminal purpose of disregarding its consequences, whether in the present or in the future, and the great mass of American white citizens should still be so mad as to sustain them in their heedless career of forcing negro supremacy over white men, why then "farewell, a long farewell," to constitutional liberty on this continent, and the glorious form of government bequeathed to us by our fathers. . . . God's law is higher than man's law. Man's puny statutes cannot repeal or nullify the immutable ordinances of the Almighty. Those whom God has separated let no man join together. . . .

Who would have dreamed fifteen years ago [that] African freedmen, of the lowest type of ignorance and brutality, would rule a sovereign State of the Union, and be the arbiters of the rights and property of a race who have ruled the destinies of nations ever since government was known among men? Such a state of things may last so long as the party shall last which had the power and audacity to inaugurate it, and no longer. . . .

Thousands of republicans, even now, hate him [the Negro] for his arrogance in the ready self-assertion of his new found rights and privileges. . . .

The condition of things in South Carolina, we dare assert, is without a parallel in the history of any people of any civilization. . . . Barbaric vengeance never went so far, never so violated the natural fitness of things, as to place the slave over his former master, the arbiter of that master's rights, by way of retribution for his former servitude, even where master and slave were of the same race, or at least of the same color. . . .

The first prominent cause of public disturbance, of which these carpet-bag patriots were the authors, was a most thorough and secret organization of the negroes, in all the counties of the State, into Loyal Leagues, in many instances armed and adopting all the formula of signs, pass-words, and grips, of an oath-bound secret organization. Who does not know, who has any knowledge at all of the negro's nature, that in an organization like this, headed by dishonest and unscrupulous white men, that the negro would be a mere blind and dumb machine in their hands? . . . The dumb mule on whose back he vaingloriously rides to the polls might just as well vote as his rider, under such circumstances, for there would be scarcely any less volition in the act of the mule than there would be on the part of the negro, at least such as we find him in South Carolina. . . .

It is some explanation, outside of the action of the carpet-baggers, of the hostile feeling entertained by the negroes of South Carolina against the white population, that the few most intelligent and influential among them, who in times of slavery were taught to read either by their masters or their masters' children, had their minds poisoned by incendiary publications distributed among them by the old anti-slavery party in the North. That class, however limited in numbers, have been the ready emissaries of the carpet-baggers, to sow hatred and vengeance in the minds of the great mass of the negro population. The sudden transition from slavery to freedom, their unexpected investiture with political power and social importance in their new relations, the tenure of office which they could not comprehend, naturally made them jealous of their former masters, and to look upon them with distrust and antipathy. . . .

The Loyal Leagues were organized in 1867, long before Ku-Kluxism reared its lawless head in South Carolina. In the convention of 1868, which adopted a State constitution under the dictates of Congress, the operations of this oath-bound League were clearly manifested. The convention was composed of one hundred and twenty-one members, seventy-two of whom were negroes and forty-nine were white men. Of the seventy-two negro members, fifty-nine paid no taxes, and were not returned on the tax-books. . . .

The riot at Chester [and other riots were] another offspring of the armed militia. The people of South Carolina might well say, so far as the troubles of 1870 are concerned, that this standing army of armed negro janizaries, as a superadded curse to the reconstructive policy of Congress,

"Brought death into the 'State' and all our woes." . . . The negroes, since their emancipation and enfranchisement . . . were determined to rule, and have ruled, the county with an iron hand, since the adoption of the new constitution. . . . It will be observed that this riot at Yorkville, although nothing serious accrued, [sic] . . . like the other riots of like character, was caused by the arming of the negroes, and their insolent and outrageous conduct after being armed. The uniformity in the conduct of the negroes, after they were organized and armed, shows very conclusively that they well understood the object of their being thus armed by the governor to the exclusion of the white men. It must be a matter of wonder to any one who has any just conception of the state of affairs in South Carolina, that a fierce and bloody war of races was avoided under the circumstances. . . .

# 11
# Northern Journalists Look at Black Reconstructionists

## THE NEW YORK TIMES

*The* New York Times *gave extended coverage, in news stories and editorials, to conditions in the South. On August 21, 1867, an editorial expressed reservations about the wisdom of conferring political rights upon Negroes, asserting: "The blacks have been made citizens before they are fit for the responsibilities of electors." It declared that blacks were not qualified to hold any but the lowest of government offices. But on April 26, 1868 the* Times *spoke favorably of the "excellent conduct" of black voters in elections in the South, which had "passed off as peaceably and quietly as though the entire population had been brought up to the duties of political life, and trained in the necessities of Republican citizenship."*

*In the following editorial (February 21, 1874), the* Times *deals with charges of corruption being made against black Reconstructionists. It agrees with the critics of the regime that conditions in South Carolina are deplorable, but says that ignorant Negroes have been duped by unscrupulous whites. It speaks favorably of efforts by black leaders to carry out reform and praises a recent speech by Robert Brown Elliott.*

Many of the negroes have been misled by white adventurers, but as a race they are not dishonest or improvident. . . . A race suddenly lifted out of bondage into control can well be pardoned many errors; and when we remember that the negroes of South Carolina fell under the influence of vicious white men, whom their instincts taught them to consider as leaders and instructors, it is not surprising that they have brought negro rule in the South into disrepute. But the fault is partly with the former dominant class, who stood haughtily aloof from affairs, and are now reaping the fruits of their mistaken policy. . . . Let them go to work to educate the negroes in honesty, thrift, and knowledge of public affairs. Only by such education can they secure any permanent relief.

In this work they will have the hearty and effectual assistance of many colored men. That this is the case is proved by a remarkable speech lately made at Columbus [sic] by Hon. R. B. Elliott, the colored member of Congress. With the courage and good sense, which have marked his entire public career, Mr. Elliott condemned the State Administration, and declared that the salvation of the Republican Party depended upon its instantly putting an end to the existing abuses. Nothing which has been said of the State Government has been more severe than the utterances of Mr. Elliott, and he was not afraid to tell the negroes that, being in the majority, they are responsible for the shame which has been brought upon the state and the ruin which is impending. And he told them plainly another truth; for he said "the national Republican Party to-day is ready to cut aloof upon the slightest provocation from the corruption now existing in the South." But what is of more consequence, he told the negroes that the remedy is in their own hands, and they must apply it. They must reform all abuses. . . . The influence of this speech for good must be very great, and it is not too much to say that in making it Mr. Elliott has rendered a public service of the very highest importance.

Let all honest men of all parties and colors now side with Mr. Elliott, and the purification of the State can soon be accomplished. . . .

## JAMES S. PIKE

*The relatively objective treatment black Reconstructionists received in the* New York Times *was not characteristic of much of the journalism of the period. The best known and most influential journalistic account is James S. Pike's* The Prostrate State: South Carolina Under Negro Government. *Pike, who was a correspondent of the* New York Tribune, *had always been racist and anti-Negro, even while opposing slavery and slaveholders. He was also strongly opposed to the Grant regime, and, by painting a dark picture of Republican misrule in South Carolina, hoped to discredit the national administration.*

*Pike's account is sensational, but much of the book is repeti-*

*tious. I have tried to excerpt representative portions dealing with blacks. The reader will recognize certain contradictions. Most of the time Pike makes sweeping generalizations about the depravity and corruption of black Reconstructionists; at times, however, he speaks favorably of their ability and cites examples of competence.*[24]

In the place of this old aristocratic society stands the rude form of the most ignorant democracy that mankind ever saw, invested with the functions of government. It is the dregs of the population habilitated in the robes of their intelligent predecessors, and asserting over them the rule of ignorance and corruption, through the inexorable machinery of a majority of numbers. It is barbarism overwhelming civilization by physical force. It is the slave rioting in the halls of his master, and putting that master under his feet. And, though it is done without malice and without vengeance, it is nevertheless none the less completely and absolutely done. Let us approach nearer and take a closer view. We will enter the House of Representatives. Here sit one hundred and twenty-four members. Of these, twenty-three are white men, representing the remains of the old civilization. These are good-looking, substantial citizens. . . .

Deducting the twenty-three members referred to, who comprise the entire strength of the opposition, we find one hundred and one remaining. Of this one hundred and one, ninety-four are colored, and seven are their white allies. Thus the blacks outnumber the whole body of whites in the House more than three to one. . . . As things stand, the body is almost literally a Black Parliament, and it is the only one on the face of the earth which is the representative of a white constituency and the professed exponent of an advanced type of modern civilization. But the reader will find almost any portraiture inadequate to give a vivid idea of the body, and enable him to comprehend the complete metamorphosis of the South Carolina Legislature, without observing its details. The Speaker is black, the Clerk is black, the door-keepers are black, the little pages are black, the chairman of the Ways and Means is black, and the chaplain is coal-black. At some of the desks sit

24. James S. Pike, *The Prostrate State: South Carolina Under Negro Government* (New York, 1874), pp. 12–15, 17, 19–20, 32–35, 46, 49, 87, 110–11.

colored men whose types it would be hard to find outside of Congo; whose costume, visages, attitudes, and expression, only befit the forecastle of a buccaneer. . . .

One of the things that first strike a casual observer in this negro assembly is the fluency of debate, if the endless chatter that goes on there can be dignified with this term. The leading topics of discussion are all well understood by the members, as they are of a practical character, and appeal directly to the personal interests of every legislator, as well as to those of his constituents. When an appropriation bill is up to raise money to catch and punish the Ku-klux, they know exactly what it means. They feel it in their bones. So, too, with educational measures. The free school comes right home to them; then the business of arming and drilling the black militia. They are eager on this point. Sambo can talk on these topics and those of a kindred character, and their endless ramifications, day in and day out. There is no end to his gush and babble. The intellectual level is that of a bevy of fresh converts at a negro camp meeting. . . .

But underneath all this shocking burlesque upon legislative proceedings, we must not forget that there is something very real to this uncouth and untutored multitude. It is not all sham, nor all burlesque. They have a genuine interest and a genuine earnestness in the business of the assembly which we are bound to recognize and respect, unless we would be accounted shallow critics. . . . Shall we, then, be too critical over the spectacle? Perhaps we might more wisely wonder that they can do so well in so short a time. . . .

But who leads among this assembly of blacks and yellows? Is it the white men? By no means; Sambo has already outgrown that.

There is a strong disposition, among the old whites of the State, to say and believe that it is the white blood in the negro race which is managing affairs in the new regime. . . . Let us look about the Legislature and see how this is. The man who uniformly discharges his duties in the most unassuming manner and in the best taste, is the chaplain of the House. He is coal-black. In the dignities and proprieties of his office, in what he says, and, still better, in what he omits to say, he might be profitably studied as a model by the white political parsons who so often officiate in Congress. Take the chairman of the House Committee of Ways and Means. He is another full-black man. By his position, he has charge of the most important business of the House. He was selected for his solid qualities, and he seems always to conduct himself with discretion. Two of the best speakers in the House are quite black. . . . Go into the Senate. It is not too much to say that the leading man of the Republican party in that body is Beverly Nash, a man wholly black. He is apparently consulted more and appealed to more, in the business of the body, than any man in it. It is admitted by his white opposition colleagues that he has more native ability than half the white men in the Senate. There is the Senator from Georgetown. He boasts of being a negro, and of having no fear of the white man in any respect. He evidently has no love for him. He is truculent and audacious, and has as much force and ability as any of the lighter-colored members of his race about him. He appears to be also one of the leading "strikers," and is not led, except through his interests. To say the least, none of the lighter-colored members of the race command any more consideration, or possess any more marked influence or talent, than these and other specimen blacks who might be named. So that there seems to be no reason for the conclusion that it is the white element in the negro race that is enabling this body of former slaves to discharge the functions of legislators. The full blacks are just as much entitled to the credit of what is done as the mulattoes. . . . Wherever those places [state offices] have been filled by colored men, the change has been advantageous to the State. This is notably the case in the important office of State Treasurer, who is a colored man [Francis Cardozo] educated abroad by a rich father, who lived in Charleston. But, as the Treasury of South Carolina has been so thoroughly gutted by the thieves who have hitherto had possession of the State government, there is nothing left to steal. . . .

The highest style of legislative spoliation is as well understood in the South Carolina Legislature as in any Tammany conclave that ever existed. The whites were the original teachers, but the blacks have shown themselves to be great adepts as scholars. If any one will take the trouble to watch the votes of the colored Representatives in Congress from South Carolina, he will not have to come down into this State to see the fact illustrated. Messrs. Elliott and Rainey had no scruples about marching with the white thieving phalanx and voting double back pay to themselves.

We may be surprised at the imitative capacity of the negro in his new functions, and even at his occasional exhibition of sense and shrewdness. When we expect nothing it is a surprise to get something. . . .

While we concede the existence of much that is good and even intelligent in the dense masses of the black population of South Carolina, and thoroughly sympathize with its rejoicings over its happy issue from a cruel bondage, and its hopes of a better future, it is impossible not to recognize the immense proportion of ignorance and vice that permeates the mass. . . .

With a constituency thus degraded, what are we to expect of its representatives?

The existing Legislature is already furnishing the answer. The black constituency of Charleston itself is to-day represented by men who belong in the penitentiary. The best that can be said is that the worst of these representatives are not black. But some of the lower counties have legislative specimens of black rascality that it would be hard to match in any white assembly. . . .

There are some individuals among the colored members who are so nearly white that no one would suspect colored blood in their veins. They are showy talkers of great animation of manner, with the same spread-eagle style that marks so much of the oratory of wholly white men. They are not amenable to the criticism bestowed on the average African-Americans of the body, for they talk intelligibly and intelligently.

In the Legislature there is a tendency to retrenchment and reform in such points as the expenditures in the departments, and on appropriations generally; the members had to promise this in the late canvass. But the economies are rather nominal than real, as the gross appropriations this year exceed those of the previous year.

## THE NATION

*At the end of the Civil War, the* Nation, *one of the most prestigious and most influential Northern periodicals, had been in the forefront in advocating political rights for freedmen, but it soon became disillusioned with the Reconstruction experiment. Its changing attitude toward black Reconstructionists was representative not only of the changing views of its editor, Edwin L. Godkin, but of Northern public opinion generally. On April 16, 1874, the* Nation *published an editorial, "Socialism in South Carolina," in which*

*it cited at length, with approval, the charges of corruption
and extravagance that Pike had made in* The Prostrate
State. *It declared that Negro domination was leading South
Carolina toward socialism. "It is not a question any longer,"
it declared, "about the more or less good government of the
State, or the rights of minorities, but whether the whites can
stay in the state at all." The editorial asserted that among the
South Carolina Negroes in the cities, those who had been free
before the war, there was "a good deal of intelligence, and
good conduct." But, it added, "the average intelligence among
the rest is very low—so low that they are but slightly above
the level of animals."*

*When Thomas Wentworth Higginson, who had com-
manded the famous black regiment, the Massachusetts Fifty-
Fourth, protested the language of the editorial, the* Nation
*(April 30, 1874) replied:*

Our assertion was too sweeping, and should have been confined to the class of negroes mentioned in the sentence immediately
succeeding that dwelt upon by our correspondent—namely, the
negroes of the low country, where the rice cultivation is carried on.
These, as we personally know, are just about as degraded as Mr.
Pike describes them to be; and considered in their capacity as legislators for an American State, to say that they are not much above
the level of the brute is not a departure from substantial accuracy.
And in no walk of life do they show themselves to be other than a
very degraded race of human beings. . . . But whatever his capacity, and whatever his general merits and demerits as a man, he
[the Negro] has succeeded in carrying South Carolina a long way on
the road to ruin. He has, to be sure, had the help of native Carolinians such as Governor Moses, and of imported statesmen, . . .
but it is clear that he could have done it without them, and they
could not have done it without him. We are not concerned about
the negro's place in nature, and have no sympathy with any effort
to depreciate or exalt him; but as a South Carolina legislator, he
is merely a horrible failure. . . .

## CHARLES NORDHOFF

*Charles Nordhoff, another journalist, made a trip through
the South in 1875 at the request of the editor of the* New

York Herald, *and published a book containing his observations. White less biased than Pike, Nordhoff was strongly opposed to the Grant administration and to federal intervention in the South; he had evidently made up his mind before beginning his travels that Reconstruction, especially the political participation by blacks, was a dismal failure. The book, which is addressed "To the President of the United States," asserts that the Grant administration has "failed to make the people of the Southern States contented," and that its Southern policy would have been different had Grant been able to see actual conditions as Nordhoff did.*

*Portions of the book that deal with Black Reconstructionists and the effects of Negro participation in politics follow.*[25]

### Preliminary

The following, then, are the conclusions I draw from my observations in the Cotton States: . . .

As to "intimidation," it is a serious mistake to imagine this exclusively a Democratic proceeding in the South. . . . The negroes are the most savage intimidators of all. In many localities which I visited, it was as much as a negro's life was worth to vote the Democratic ticket; and even to refuse to obey the caucus of his party caused him to be denounced as "Bolter," and to be forsaken by his friends, and even by his life or sweetheart. That there has been Democratic intimidation is undeniable; but it does not belong to the Southern Republicans to complain of it. . . .

There are no wrongs now in the South which the interference of the Federal Government under the Enforcement acts can reach. This interference is purely and only mischievous. . . .

The negroes have developed quite a genius for the lower political arts. They have among them not a few shrewd and calculating demagogues, who know as well how to "run the machine," to form a ring, and to excite the voters to their duty, as any New York City politician. Office is of course a great temptation to men used to field-work at small wages; and the moderate pay even of a juryman, with its accompanying idleness, seems very delightful to them. They have long ago discovered their numerical strength in many

25. Charles Nordhoff, *The Cotton States in the Spring and Summer of 1875* (New York, 1876), pp. 10–12, 22, 66–68, 74–75.

parts of the South, and do not hesitate to say in some places that, as they cast the votes, they ought to have the offices. At least a dozen times I came upon this saying in different places; and there are signs which show that if the present political divisions could continue, the black leaders would, in counties where the blacks predominate, in two or three years crowd all the white men out of the Republican party; or, at least, all who aspired to office. But they would not attempt this unless they felt assured of the protection of the Federal power; when they lose that reliance, every body, of both parties, says they will lose the power of cohesive action. . . .

### Louisiana

The negroes are becoming a nuisance to their corrupt white allies. Under the inspiration of Pinchback and other ambitious colored leaders, they begin to grasp after all the offices. "We have the majority," they say: "we cast the votes; the offices belong to us; we do not need you." They are ready to give judgeships to the whites; but the Legislature, the sheriffs' places, the police-juries, (county supervisors)—all the places where money is to be spent or appropriated—they demand, in those parishes where they are the majority. . . .

The real embarrassment in the future lies with Packard and Pinchback.[26] They believe in the color-line, and Pinchback is an unscrupulous, and, with his own people, a very influential, politician. The colored people, unfortunately, are very susceptible to such influences as his. They are—their best friends and most zealous supporters openly confess it—incapable of independent political action. They require a leader. . . .

Now, Pinchback understands organization. He has at this time a propagandist of his views in many parishes, and it is said he means to make himself, if he can, master of the colored vote. I believe he can not do it; but he can do much mischief. . . .

The only sure remedy, I am persuaded, lies in the absolute non-interference of the Federal power. . . . Take away the constant menace of Federal interference, and the whole body of corruptionists will at once sink out of sight, as they did in Arkansas.

Nor do I believe that any serious disorder would happen in the State. . . .

26. Stephen B. Packard was a white leader opposed to Governor Warmoth.

## Mississippi

Mississippi is, politically, in a melancholy condition. . . . Here are two examples which do not badly illustrate the state of affairs in Mississippi.

Knowing that I am interested in schools, some one in New Orleans sent me a letter of introduction to the State Superintendent of Public Instruction here—a colored man named Cardozo. On asking for him I found he had gone to Vicksburg "to look after an indictment" found against him; and when I myself went there, I discovered that Cardozo was not merely indicted, but, as an indignant Republican told me, "shingled all over with indictments" for embezzlement and fraud, and likely, if justice is done, presently to be sent to State-prison. What a lovely and improving sight for the children of the State, white and black!

Yet this man is one of Governor Ames's confidential and influential advisers.

Here is the other side. The postmaster, ex-Senator Pease, while I was in Vicksburg, was stopped in the street by a person who, I was assured, is "one of the most respectable citizens" of the place, who said to him in a loud voice, "I hear, sir, by God, that you are going to appoint a damned nigger to be a clerk in your post-office!" Pease replied that he certainly was going to appoint a colored man to a clerkmanship. "Then, sir, I tell you it's a damned outrage, and this community won't stand it, sir!" said this "most respectable citizen" in a blustering tone. Pease replied, "You will have to stand it," which is perfectly true. And as they have a colored sheriff already in Vicksburg, and colored officials in many counties, this bluster seems to be as foolish as it is wicked. . . .

The next day's Vicksburg *Herald,* the Democratic organ remarks:

"Pease was remonstrated with yesterday upon the assignment of a negro to the ladies' window. A gentleman modestly suggested that the men of Vicksburg would not submit to have a negro assigned to the duty of waiting on their wives and daughters at the post-office, when the insolent scoundrel replied, 'They will have to stand it!' The appointment is a deliberate insult to the ladies of this city. . . ."

The colored man whom Mr. Pease has made clerk in the post-office is a young man of education, acknowledged integrity, and quiet, gentlemanly demeanor, whom several Democrats praised to me. The hack-driver who objected to him never objects to taking a fare from a negro, and a citizen of Vicksburg told me he had seen him repeatedly driving negro prostitutes about the town. The "most respectable citizen" is agent for a steamboat line, daily sells tickets to colored people, and never refuses their money. The whole affair would be a farce, if it were not so likely to become a tragedy.

# 12

## British Travelers Look at
## Black Reconstructionists

**ROBERT SOMERS**

*The novelty of the political and social changes in
the South during Reconstruction attracted a number of foreign visitors. Among them was Robert Somers, an Englishman
who traveled throughout the South in 1870–71 and wrote a
book describing conditions. He is somewhat less prejudiced
and less superficial than many observers. Below are portions
of his chapters on South Carolina and Louisiana, in which
he gives his impressions of black Reconstructionists.*[27]

### South Carolina

Ask what the system of rule is, and the reply will uniformly be
that it is "nigger rule," which is in one sense true. The negroes are
more numerous than the whites in South Carolina. . . . There not
being "carpet-baggers" or "scalawags" enough in the State to fill
all the seats in the Legislature, the negroes have largely returned
men of their own race to watch over "laws and learning," and
"ships, colonies, and commerce," at the Capitol. The House of
Representatives consists of 80 coloured men and 44 whites, and the
Senate of 11 coloured men and 20 whites—there being one seat
vacant just now. The white people of South Carolina are thus practically disfranchised, and a proletariat Parliament has been constituted, the like of which could not be produced under the widest
suffrage in any part of the world save in some of these Southern
States. The outcry of misgovernment, extravagant expenditure,
jobbery, and corruption is both loud and general. The negroes are
declared to be the dupes of designing men, comparative strangers
to the State, whose object is simply to fill their pockets out of the
public spoil. Political charges are not minced in South Carolina.

27. Robert Somers, *The Southern States Since the War, 1870–1* (London and
New York, 1871), pp. 41–43, 226–28.

There is room, indeed, to hope for a good deal of exaggeration. The exclusion of the superior part of the population from all influence in public affairs must of itself tend to magnify the enormity of everything enormous, and to distort everything not quite square that is done. . . .

I allude at this length to political affairs in South Carolina, because it is very obvious that a system of government resting almost wholly on the votes of the negroes is not a desirable state of affairs as regards either the State itself or the general interests of the Union. It destroys confidence in the integrity and stability of the Administration, prevents the investment of money, and renders impossible that hearty co-operation of the public authorities with the substantial people of the State which is so essential to the interests of all classes of the community.

### Louisiana

Almost the first question put to a stranger, is, whether he has seen "the Negro Legislature?" and the Legislative Assembly of the State, as at present constituted, seems to be regarded much in the light of a joke by most of the citizens.

I went to see the Legislature of Louisiana. . . . Within the Chamber itself were seated in semi-circle round the Speaker's chair, with little fixed desks and drawers full of papers before them, a body of men as sedate and civilized in appearance as a convention of miners' delegates in Scotland or the North of England. On close inspection, a few Africans were visible, but yellow men seemed to predominate. The Senate differed little in general aspect or composition, but was presided over by Lieutenant-Governor Dunn, a really black man as far as could be seen in the shadow, and was being addressed by an honourable white Senator of an intellectual cast of head and face, who appears to have gained more notoriety than all the rest by marrying a black woman. . . .

It is strange, abnormal, and unfit that a negro Legislature should deal, as the Legislature of Louisiana has been dealing, with the gravest commercial and financial interests, dispensing not only the State taxes and patronage, but the levees of the Mississippi, and the sugar sheds, warehousing, and cattle marketing of New Orleans to private companies, with unlimited powers of compulsion and taxation over the community of merchants, planters, and white people of business and industry, who, though a numerical majority of the population, have as little power in the government as if they were inhabitants of another sphere, and are forced to speak of it only as a grim jest, or as a playful though melancholy jibe. . . .

The Governor of Louisiana, Warmoth, is a young man of spirit and ability, who came down to New Orleans at the close of the war, and by dexterously "fugling" the negro vote, got himself advanced to this high position, in which he seems to be growing wiser if richer. . . . The outcry against him has been loud and deep; . . . It is not uncommon to hear in New Orleans that Dunn, the negro Lieutenant-Governor, is a more trustworthy man than his superior in office; and while there is no doubt that the fair Desdemona of the State has been foully wronged, it seems a puzzle whether Othello or Iago be the more to blame. . . .

### WILLIAM HEPWORTH DIXON

*The most blatantly racist of the books by travelers is* White Conquest, *by William Hepworth Dixon. In the following selection, Dixon is giving his version of the political situation in Louisiana and an account of the election of P. B. S. Pinchback to the United States Senate and the contest over seating him. He pictures Pinchback as a crude, tobacco-chewing rogue.*[28]

A Negro, named Pinchback, known familiarly as Pinch, offered his services to [Governor William P.] Kellogg—at a price. This Pinch, a bustling fellow, had been a steward on board a steamboat, and afterwards an usher in a gambling den; but, like others of his tribe, he found that politics paid him better than washing basins, keeping doors, and dodging the police. As senator for a negro district he happened to have served some weeks in office as successor to Lieutenant-governor Dunn. His time was up; but in America titles cling to men for life. Once a professor

---

28. William Hepworth Dixon, *White Conquest,* 2 vols. (London, 1876), **II,** 11–14, 17–18, 104–7.

always a professor; once a Lieutenant-governor always a Lieutenant-governor. Though lost to office, Pinch had still a handle to his name.

This man seemed worth his salt, and Kellogg came to terms with him. Pinch was to upset Warmoth. If he succeeded, he was to be Acting Governor for a few days, to have a large sum of money, and, if Norton could be set aside, to go as senator to Washington. . . . Seldom in either history or fiction have grotesqueness and absurdity been carried to such lengths. . . .

Kellogg contrived that Pinch should be proposed as the republican candidate for Senator. Norton gave way for him; and it was hoped that his election to the Senate might help to cover his illegal acts. . . .

For four or five weeks Pinch ruled the State, as Jacques rules his duchy in the "Honeymoon." Jesters squibbed him as King Pinch, His Nigger Majesty, Lord Paper Collar, and Marquis of Pomade. . . . At length, his reign was over, and he handed the State House and the Great Seal to Kellogg; taking as his price the title of Governor, the Senatorship in Washington, and all the openings and emoluments of that chair.

Pinchback's entry in the Senate, where he claimed a seat among the Shermans and Wilsons, Boutwells and Camerons, grave and conscript fathers of the republic, raised a storm which has not yet subsided, though twenty-two months have passed since he first laid his credentials on the table of that house.

A committee was appointed by the Senate to investigate his claim. . . .

*Dixon visits the Louisiana legislature, which is again considering Pinchback's claims to the Senate seat.*

On passing to the Upper House, we find a tall, pale Negro, with a small head and dissipated face, presiding over fifteen Black and thirteen White senators, who are debating whether they shall or shall not read the Senators in Washington, a lesson by sending Pinchback up again as State Senator for Louisiana? This pale and dissipated Negro is the Hon. Caesar C. Antoine, Lieutenant-governor of the State, sitting in the chair by virtue of his office. No Conservative senators are present.

Caesar C. Antoine is an African of pure blood, though he is not so dark as many of his brethren on the Niger and the Senegal. Small in stature and weak in frame, his only strength appears to lie in a feminine sort of shrewdness. Antoine was a porter in the Custom House. Before he took to politics he could hardly get his pay, yet, having a place under Government, he found the way open to public life. His rise was rapid. From the bench of a porter he passed to the chair of Lieutenant-governor. He was a servant of clerks; he is the master of senators. Since the Caliph made his porter a pasha, no man of his calling has been raised to so high a place. It was a golden chance. Apart from accidents, Antoine is not a man who could have risen. . . .

The Negro senators agree that the White fellows in Washington are impertinent in rejecting Pinch. He is the martyr of his skin. Those White fellows talk about his character. What right have they to pry into a gentleman's private life? They prate about Governor Kellogg's election not being valid. What right have those fellows to review a State election in Louisiana? Pinch shall go back. Pinch is their choice. Pinch shall sit in their name under the marble dome, among the chief sages of the commonwealth!

On going with Antoine into Kellogg's cabinet we encounter Pinch. The Negro is in high feather, for the Negro senators have just affirmed once more his election to the State Senatorship, and Antoine has brought his credentials for the Governor to sign and seal. Got up in paper collar and pomade, Pinch smiles and smirks, and sickens you with his bows and scrapes. You think of giving him twenty cents. Kellogg appears to loathe the fellow, yet he cannot well refuse his name and seal. Who knows with what reserve he signs? Pinch watches him with eager eyes, chewing his quid, and spattering the walls and carpets. Ach! The scene is rich in comedy. Having got his papers signed, Pinch whips up his satchel, sticks a fresh quid in his mouth, and leaves the room with Antoine, the two Negroes going out arm in arm, strutting and sniggering through admiring crowds. "Dat Nig is some," one fellow cries. "You bet?" asks another. "Golly," says a third, "dat Nig is ole Pinch!" And so the dusky hero vanishes from our sight.

"It is a farce," says Governor Kellogg. "Pinchback is no more

senator now than he was before. He goes on a fool's errand, but
these coloured children must be humoured. When he reaches
Washington they will find out their mistake."

### Another View of Pinchback

> *The Senate finally decided on March 8, 1876, by a vote of
> 32 to 29, not to seat Pinchback. But they later voted to pay
> him and his opponent salary and travel expenses up to the
> time of the termination of the contest. While the Senate was
> considering Pinchback's case, the following article was pub-
> lished in the* New York Commercial Advertiser. *It presents a
> very different picture of Pinchback from that portrayed by
> William Hepworth Dixon.*[29]

Today, on motion of Senator Morton, the Senate agreed to
go at "Pinch," *pro* and *con,* and sit without intermission until they
have made him a skylark in the air or a turtle in the mud. The
contest will be fierce. . . . McCreery, Senator from Kentucky, declares, privately, in that pastoral phraseology proverbially peculiar
to the blue grass Democrats, that he "will give that nigger some
sleepless nights before he gets his seat." . . . Pinchback glides
around the Chamber like a bronze Mephistopheles, smiling sar-
donically, and buzzing his supporters.

He is a trained politician, if he does not prove to be a statesman,
and has "counted noses" until he avers himself certain of eleven
majority on a full vote—and he is too good a "whip" not to have
all his friends on hand when it comes to a vote. In fact the mad
obstinacy and devilish cruelties of the White League in the South
recently, have made Pinchback's support a party measure, and unless indisputable evidences of fraud are brought against him by
better authority than New Orleans pimps, thugs, and traitors, the
North will assuredly accept the loyal Negro in preference to the pos-
sibility of a white rebel. Aside from the political view of the
question, Pinchback's presence in the Senate is not open to the
smallest objection, except the old Bourbon war-whoops of color.
[*sic*] He is about thirty-seven years of age, not darker than an

29. Reprinted in William J. Simmons, *Men of Mark* (Cleveland, 1887), pp. 769–
71.

Arab, less so than Kanaka. Like Lord Tomnoddy, "his hair is straight, but his whiskers curl." His features are regular, just perceptibly African, his eyes intensely black and brilliant, with a keen, restless, glance. His most repellent [sic] point is a sardonic smile which, hovering continuously over his lips, gives him an evil look, undeniably handsome as the man is. It seems as though the scorn which must rage within him, at the sight of the dirty, ignorant men from the South who affect to look down upon him on account of his color, finds play imperceptibly about his lips.

His manner is reserved but polite, exhibiting a modesty rarely seen in a successful politician—a model indeed of good breeding to those Texas and Louisiana Yahoos who shout "nigger, nigger, nigger," in default of common sense or logic. Mr. Pinchback is the best dressed Southern man we have had in Congress from the South since the days when gentlemen were Democrats. . . .

#### SIR GEORGE CAMPBELL

*Sir George Campbell, another Englishman, who visited the South soon after the collapse of the last of the Republican state regimes, presents a more objective and more balanced judgment of black Reconstructionists than some earlier writers.*[30]

During the last dozen years the negroes have had a very large share of political education. Considering the troubles and the ups and downs that they have gone through, it is, I think, wonderful how beneficial this education has been to them, and how much these people, so lately in the most debased condition of slavery, have acquired independent ideas, and, far from lapsing into anarchy, have become citizens with ideas of law and property and order. The white serfs of European countries took hundreds of years to rise to the level which these negroes have attained in a dozen. . . .

As politicians some of them have done fairly well, and are now good and popular representatives of their race; but I don't think any of them have made a great mark. The politics of the Southern

30. Sir George Campbell, *White and Black. The Outcome of a Visit to the United States* (New York, 1879), pp. 131, 137, 172–73, 176, 180.

States, while negro majorities prevailed, seem to have been in reality entirely under the guidance of the white "Carpet-baggers." . . .

Partly owing to the greater numerical preponderance of the blacks, and partly to the less disposition of the whites to accept measures of moderation and compromise, the black predominance in the Legislature and the Carpet-bag rule were carried further and lasted much longer in South Carolina than in the surrounding States. The great majority of the legislators were blacks; and though some of them were fair representative men, with some education, no doubt most of them were absurdly ignorant . . . and there was some colour for the nickname of the "Monkey House," which their enemies applied to the Assembly. They, however, indulged in no violent class-legislation, but were very completely guided by the white men who had obtained the government—principally Northern Carpet-baggers. Whatever violence and disturbance there was (and there was a good deal), was not on the part of the black majority, but of the white minority, who, instead of trying constitutional methods to regain power, preferred Ku Klux organisations and such violent methods, committing many murders and creating much terror. . . .

When I went to South Carolina I thought that there at least I must find great social disturbances; and in South Carolina I went to the county of Beaufort, the blackest part of the State in point of population, and that in which black rule has been most complete and has lasted longest. It has the reputation of being a sort of black paradise, and, *per contra,* I rather expected a sort of white hell. There I thought I should see a rough Liberia, where the blacks ruled roughshod over the whites. To my great surprise I found exactly the contrary. At no place that I have seen are the relations of the two races better and more peaceable. . . . Here the blacks still control the elections and send their representatives to the State Assembly; but though they elect to the county and municipal offices they by no means elect blacks only. . . .

"Well, then," I have gone on to ask, "did the black Legislatures make bad law?" My informants could not say that they did. . . . What, then, is the practical evil of which complaint is made? The answer is summed up in the one word "corruption." . . . In South Carolina I was given the report of the Committee of Investigation disclosing terrible things, and said to be most impartial and conclusive. The general result was to leave in one's mind the belief that undoubtedly a very great deal of pilfering and corruption had gone on, but the tone of the report was far too much that of an indictment, rather than of a judgment, to satisfy me that it could safely be accepted in block. . . .

On the whole, then, I am inclined to believe that the period of Carpet-bag rule was rather a scandal than a very permanent injury. The black men used their victory with moderation, although the women were sometimes dangerous, and there was more pilfering than plunder on a scale permanently to cripple the State.

## PART THREE

# BLACK RECONSTRUCTIONISTS IN HISTORY

# 13
## Views of an Old Abolitionist

*In this selection, part of a symposium on Negro suffrage published in the* North American Review *in 1879, Wendell Phillips, the long-time abolitionist, vigorously defends black Reconstructionists and their legislative records. He asserts that the white South feared the success, not the failure of Negro suffrage. He places responsibility for any misrule on the whites who shirked their political duties during Reconstruction, and blames the federal government for failure to take more decisive action to protect blacks, and for failure to insure their economic independence by guaranteeing them land.[1]*

Negro suffrage has not been a failure. Only the merest surface judgment would so consider it. Though his voting has been crippled and curtailed throughout a large part of the South during half the time he has been entitled to vote, the negro has given the best evidence of his fitness for suffrage by valuing it at its full worth. Every investigation of Southern fraud has shown him less purchasable than the white man. He has wielded his vote with as much honor and honesty—to claim the very least—as any class of Southern whites; even of those intellectually his superiors. For nine fearful years he has clung to the Republican party (which at least promised to protect him) as no white class, North or South, would have done. Want and starvation he has manfully defied, and asserted his rights till shot down in their very exercise. . . .

In law-making the negro has nothing to fear when compared

1. *North American Review,* 128 (March, 1879), 257–60.

with the whites. Taking away the laws which white cunning and hate have foisted into the statute-book, the legislation of the South since the rebellion may challenge comparison with that of any previous period. This is all due to the negro. The educated white Southerner skulked his responsibility. Either the negro himself devised those laws, or he was wise enough to seek and take the good advice of his friends. . . . They say negro Legislatures doubled the taxes. Well, there were double the number of children to be educated, and double the number of men (one half of them previously *things*) to be governed and cared for.

The South owes to negro labor and to legislation under negro rule all the prosperity she now enjoys—prosperity secured in spite of white ignorance and hate. The negro is to-day less ignorant, superstitious, and helpless than the same class of Southern white men; yes, than a class of whites supposed to be immeasurably his superiors.

The South would not have disfranchised the negro if his suffrage had been a failure. Its success is what she fears and hates. When lawless and violent men attack any element of law and civilization, and can only succeed by destroying it, does not that very assault prove the value and efficiency of that obstacle to their lawless purpose?

Negro suffrage gave the helm to the Republican party when it represented a principle—that was intelligent. It stood firmer against bribery than other Southerners—that was honest. It vindicated the negro's fitness for legislation—that scattered the fogs about negro inferiority. It educated the negro more and more every day, and was fast bringing him to a level with the whites of the best class—that was death to Southern dreams of future rule and treason.

In those States where either circumstances or the nation have secured the negro anything like fair play, his suffrage has been a marked success.

If negro suffrage has been in any particular or respect a failure, it has not been the negro's fault, nor in consequence of any want or lack in him. If it has failed to secure all the good it might have produced, this has been because of cowardice, selfishness, and want of statesmanship on the part of the Government of the United States. . . .

Negro suffrage has not, therefore, been a failure, even in any trivial degree, from any lack of courage, intelligence, or honesty on his part. And let it be remembered how early the Ku-klux assaulted him; how incessant have been the attacks upon him all these years; how brave and unquailing has been his resistance. Let it be kept in mind also that, meanwhile, one half of the journals of these forty States have been against him; and seven-tenths of the Federal officers and the whole organized power of the white South. All this while the negro has accumulated property, risen in position, advanced marvelously in education, outrunning the white man in this race. He has proved himself equal to any post he has gained. On the floor of Congress the Southern white has more than once quailed before negro logic, sarcasm, and power of retort. . . .

After the negro has used his vote as honestly and intelligently as the average Northerner, and more bravely, shall we withdraw it because the caste prejudice, that hates him and dreads it, lives "unharmoniously" in its sight? . . .

Every man sees now what very few saw ten years ago (and I am glad I was one of those few, ridiculed as we then were), that to enfranchise the negro, without doing all the nation could to insure his independence, was a wrong to him and disastrous to us.

Treason should have been punished by confiscating its landed property. . . . Land should have been divided among the negroes, forty acres to each family, and tools—poor pay for the unpaid toil of six generations on that very soil. Mere emancipation without any compensation to the victim was pitiful atonement for ages of wrong. Planted on his own land, sure of bread—instead of being merely a wages-slave—the negro's suffrage would have been a very different experiment.

# 14
## Apologists for the White South

### JOHN SCHREINER REYNOLDS

*Around the turn of the century, numerous local historians published accounts of the Reconstruction era in which they pictured orgies of misrule under "negro domination" and glorified the white "Redeemers" who overthrew the Republican regimes.* Reconstruction in South Carolina, 1865–1877, *by John Schreiner Reynolds, from which the following selection is taken, is one of the better examples. Reynolds made extensive use of public documents and other published sources, but his intense prejudice against black Reconstructionists is obvious, as seen, for example, in his description of some of the black leaders.*[2]


"Daddy" Cain was a Northern negro preacher who got that soubriquet by his efforts to mimic the ways of the old-time Southern negro. For some time he edited in Charleston his paper, called the *Missionary Record,* the columns of which often contained matter of a most incendiary character—appeals to the passions of the negroes, coupled with outrageous abuse of the white people. For some of the bloodshed in this State during the Reconstruction period "Daddy" Cain and his *Missionary Record* were in part responsible. Though sometimes denouncing the corrupt practices of his party, his actual affiliation was generally with the thieves. He stumped the State in advocacy of the election of Frank Moses for Governor. The case of Cain is thus referred to in order to point out the influence, in some degree, once exerted by the African Methodist Episcopal Church on the side of dishonesty and discord in South Carolina. . . .

2. John Schreiner Reynolds, *Reconstruction in South Carolina, 1865–1877* (Columbia, S. C., 1905), pp. 109–10, 128, 286, 333, 503–4, 514.

Associate Justice Hoge having resigned, the Legislature elected in his place Jonathan J. Wright, the negro senator from Beaufort. Wright was a native of Pennsylvania, and thirty-three years old. He graduated from a high school in Lancaster, and then studied law for two years in Montrose. He was admitted to the bar in Susquehanna County—being the first negro licensed to practice in that State. He had practiced only four years before coming to South Carolina and when elected was practically without experience in any of her courts. No white man of his attainments and experience (except, of course, his immediate predecessor, Hoge) could have been elected to the bench of South Carolina. He was chosen because he was a negro—and most of the Democratic members of the Legislature thought it well to vote for him as against Whipper. It was generally believed that Wright frequently had the help of a capable lawyer in preparing his opinions. Some of those papers bear evidence of having been written entire by some good lawyer —being in their language, arrangement and citations manifestly beyond Wright's capacity. He remained on the bench till, in 1877, he resigned under impeachment for official misconduct. . . .

[Robert B.] Elliott had been a conspicuous figure in South Carolina politics ever since the meeting of the Constitutional Convention called under the Reconstruction acts. He was violent, sometimes almost incendiary, in his appeals to the negroes to stand by their race, and held extreme views on all questions of civil rights—meaning social equality. He soon became a leader among the negroes and was courted by most of the white men who called themselves Republicans. He was the first chairman of the House Committee on Railroads, and in that capacity was believed to have received large bribes from John J. Patterson for helping on the schemes for the acquisition of the Blue Ridge Railroad and the Greenville and Columbia Railroad. On the occasion of the attempt to impeach Governor Scott, Elliott received one bribe of more than $10,000 and, according to common report at the time, considerable sums besides. He was generally considered utterly corrupt, and his influence, in whatever sphere he had opportunity, was always on the side of the robbers. He was directly responsible for some of the race troubles in South Carolina. His personal character, aside from his conduct in office or in politics, was of a low order—im-

moral to an extent difficult to understand in a man of his education
and his prominence in the Republican party. Though very mouthy
he was generally accounted a coward. As a product of Reconstruction in South Carolina Robert B. Elliott must be classed among the
very lowest and the very worst. . . .

R. B. Elliott, already noticed, illustrated the somewhat rare combination presented by the knave in the person of an educated man
apparently having every incentive to lead an honest life. Elliott
was unquestionably the ablest negro that figured in the Reconstruction period in South Carolina—an excellent speaker and a fine presiding officer. Yet he was officially corrupt and personally without
any regard for decency or morality.

In this connection it is only fair to note the fact that every objection of the white people of South Carolina to the establishment of
the Constitution of 1868—every prediction of bad results to follow
—was amply justified by the course of the negro government at
various stages of its existence. Bad as it was, conditions would
have been far worse but for the coolness, bravery and forbearance
of the white people acting under the advice of wise and patriotic
leaders.

It has been charged that the deliverance of South Carolina from
negro rule and from the infamies continuously incident thereto
was accomplished by unlawful means—by force or fraud or both.
Whatever may be said of the methods alleged to have been used
by the whites in the campaign of 1876, it must also be said that the
conduct of the negroes, incited by their leaders, was quite as
bad. . . .

The personnel of the convention held to organize the Republican party of South Carolina, as already given, was an index to
that of every similar body assembled in that State during the period
of negro rule—the Constitutional Convention, the General Assembly and every convention of that party. The ruling characteristic
of each of these bodies was its irresponsibility. Dominated either
by native whites conscious of having incurred the displeasure of
their race or by "carpet-baggers" who never had any standing among
that race, or by smart negroes most of whom were unscrupulous,
or by all of these acting together, the constituency to which these
bodies looked was the negro race exclusively—and this race incapable of forming any judgment upon the actions of men,

naturally suspicious of their former masters and stirred to hostility to these latter by the vicious counsels of political tutors. . . .

Such being the character of the negro government of South Carolina, such the motives and conduct of its agents, it naturally became a "stench in the nostrils of decent people" and a disgrace to the country. The Federal bayonets removed, the power of the thieves destroyed, the so-called government fell to pieces of its own imbecility, came to nought of its own all-pervading corruption. Negro domination had proven as well an injury to the black race as an offense to the white—an experiment always doomed to failure— the device of those who, in the name of freedom and justice, had inaugurated and sustained a government that was never worthy of the name.

### REMINISCENCES OF A WHITE MISSISSIPPIAN

*W. H. Hardy, a lawyer and railroad builder who was also a captain in the Confederate army, recalls James Lynch, the black Reconstructionist who served as secretary of state.*[3]

Jim Lynch alone deserves especial notice in this paper. He was a dark mulatto, born and raised in Pennsylvania; he was highly educated and was a Methodist preacher, and was sent down to this State by the Northern Methodists as a missionary to the negroes. He was a remarkable man. He was of medium height, broad-shouldered, with a superb head and sparkling brown eyes; his hair was black and glossy and stood in profusion on his head between a kink and a curl. He was a great orator; fluent and graceful, he stirred his great audiences as no other man did or could do. He was the idol of the negroes, who would come from every point of the compass and for miles, on foot, to hear him speak. He rarely spoke to less than a thousand, and often two to five thousand. He swayed them with as much ease as a man would sway a peacock feather with his right hand. They yelled and howled, and laughed, and cried, as he willed. I have heard him paint the horrors of slavery (as they existed in his imagination) in pathetic tones of sympathy till the tears would roll down his cheeks, and every negro

3. W. H. Hardy, "Recollections of Reconstruction in East and Southeast Mississippi," *Publications of the Mississippi Historical Society* 9 (1901), 126–27.

in the audience would be weeping; then wiping briskly away his tears, he would break forth into hosannas for the blessings of emancipation, and every negro in the audience would break forth in the wildest shouts. There was a striking peculiarity about this shouting. Imagine one or two thousand negroes standing *en masse* in a semi-circle facing the speaker; not a sound to be heard except the sonorous voice of the speaker, whose tones were as clear and resonant as a silver bell; and of a sudden, every throat would be wide open, and a spontaneous shout in perfect unison would arise, and swell, and subside as the voice of one man; then for a moment a deadly silence would follow, and every eye would be fixed on the speaker as he resumed, until all of a sudden the mighty shout would rise again, and again, and so on, at intervals for a period of from one to three hours. The writer has stood transfixed to the spot, and listened to him, and observed the masses so completely under his influence, and how, as one man, they would all shout together; no one gave the cue, but all together, and the rhythmic cadences were in perfect unison. I could not understand it; but in the light of the discoveries of the laws of psychic phenomena, I am now sure that it was done by the hypnotic power or influence of the speaker. Doctor Hudson, in his work on the *Law of Psychic Phenomena*, states that all great orators possess hypnotic power, and by this power sway their audiences.

Lynch always spoke out doors, as no house could hold his audiences, and always spoke in daylight. He was a great coward and could never be persuaded to speak at night.

He was elected to the office of Secretary of State, . . . He died before his term of office expired, and before reaching the full meridian of his manhood. The mongrel legislature appropriated two thousand five hundred dollars for a monument to his memory, and it is a singular fact that he is the only man to whose memory a monument was ever erected in Mississippi by legislative appropriation.

### WALTER L. FLEMING

*Walter L. Fleming was one of the most distinguished members of the Dunning school of historians. His volume,* Civil War and Reconstruction in Alabama, *published in 1905, is a good example of the way white historians of the early*

*twentieth century looked at black Reconstructionists. The
following portions of his account of the elections of delegates
to the 1868 constitutional convention and of the role of blacks
in the convention illustrate his assumption of Negro inferiority and his conviction that blacks were gullible, ignorant
dupes of unscrupulous whites.*[4]

The elections, early in October, were the most remarkable
in the history of the state. For the first time the late slaves were to
vote, while many of their former masters could not. . . . To control the negro vote the Radicals devoted all the machinery of
registration and election, the Union League and the Freedmen's
Bureau. The chiefs of the League sent agents to the plantation
negroes, who were showing some indifference to politics, with strict
orders to go and vote. They were told that if they did not vote they
would be reenslaved and their wives would be made to work the
roads and quit wearing hoopskirts. . . . At Clayton the negroes
were driven to town and camped the day before election began.
There was firing of guns all night. Early the next morning the
local leaders formed the negroes into companies and regiments and
marched them, armed with shotguns, muskets, pistols, and knives
to the courthouse, where the only polling place for the county was
situated. The first day there were about three thousand of them,
of all ages from fifteen to eighty years of age, and no whites were
allowed to approach the sacred voting place. When drawn up in
line each man was given a ticket by the League representatives, and
no negro was allowed to break ranks until all were safely corralled
into the courthouse square. . . .

The registration lists were not referred to except when a white
man offered to vote. Most of the negroes had strange ideas of what
voting meant. It meant freedom, for one thing, if they voted the
Radical ticket and Slavery if they did not. One negro at Selma held
up a blue (Conservative) ticket and cried out, "No land! no mules!
no votes! slavery again!" Then holding up a red (Radical) ticket
he shouted, "Forty acres of land! a mule! freedom! votes! equal of
white man!" Of course he voted the red ticket. . . .

The delegates elected to the convention were a motley crew—

4. Walter L. Fleming, *Civil War and Reconstruction in Alabama* (New York,
1905), pp. 514–15, 517–18, 521–23.

white, yellow, and black—of northern men, Bureau officers, "loyalists," "rebels," who had aided the Confederacy and now perjured
themselves by taking the oath, Confederate deserters, and negroes.
. . . There were eighteen blacks. . . . Of the negro members two
could write well and were fairly well educated, half could not read
a word, and others had been taught to sign their names and that
was all. There were many negroes who could read and write, but
they were not sent to the convention. Perhaps the carpetbaggers
feared trouble from them and wanted only those whom they could
easily control. . . .

The colored delegates brought up the negro question in several
forms. First, Rapier of Canada wanted a declaration that negroes
were entitled to all the privileges and rights of citizenship in
Alabama. Then Strother of Dallas demanded that negroes be empowered to collect pay from those who held them in slavery, at
the rate of $10 a month for services rendered from January 1, 1863,
the date of the Emancipation Proclamation, to May 20, 1865. An
ordinance to this effect was actually adopted by a vote of 53 to 31.
The scalawags, as a rule, wished to prohibit intermarriage of the
races. . . . The negroes and carpetbaggers united to vote this down.
. . . Gregory (negro) of Mobile wanted all regulations, laws, and
customs wherein distinctions were made on account of color or
race to be abolished, and thus allow intermarriages. The convention refused to adopt the report providing against amalgamation.
The Mobile negroes alone seem to have been opposed to the prohibition of intermarriage. . . .

Caraway (negro) of Mobile succeeded in having an ordinance
passed directing that church property used during slavery for
colored congregations be turned over to the latter. Some of this
property was paid for by negro slaves and held in trust for them
by white trustees. Most of it, however, belonged to the planters who
erected churches for the use of their slaves. . . .

In spite of efforts to keep the question in the background, the
racial equality of the negro was demanded by one or two irrepressible Mobile mulattoes, and a discussion was precipitated. The
scalawags with few exceptions were opposed to admitting negroes
to the same privileges as whites,—in theatres, churches, on railroads and boats, and at hotels,—though they were willing to require
equal but separate accommodations for both races. . . . Rapier
(negro) of Canada said that the manner in which colored gentlemen

and ladies were treated in America was beyond his comprehension.
. . . Some of the negroes forcibly opposed the agitation of the
question on the ground that the civil and political rights of the
negro were not yet safe and should not be endangered by the agitation on the social question. . . .

### JAMES FORD RHODES

*Although he was not professionally trained, James Ford
Rhodes was one of the most respected and most impartial historians of the early twentieth century. In his monumental*
History of the United States from the Compromise of 1850,
*he showed himself strongly opposed to slavery. On most issues
he appeared to support the position of the Republican party,
but on the issue of Reconstruction his sympathies were clearly
with the white South. That he regarded blacks as inherently
inferior and their participation in politics as a disaster is
shown by the following selection dealing with Mississippi and
South Carolina.*[5]

An examination of the legislature [of Mississippi] reveals the
common blight. Thirty-six negroes were members, most of whom
had been slaves. A number could neither read nor write and, when
they drew their pay, acknowledged its receipt by making their
mark. From out this massive ignorance there rose, indeed, the occasional shape of enlightenment: a coloured minister such as Revels
the quadroon; also John R. Lynch layman and mulatto who was a
credit to his race and in 1872 made an impartial and dignified
speaker of the House. But the aspirations of most of the negroes
were as low as their life experience had been narrow.

A few examples will show how the dregs of the constituencies
had risen to the surface. The county of which Vicksburg was the
chief town sent four negroes to the legislature, that which contained
Jackson, the State capital, three; four represented Adams, the
county renowned for "its ancient aristocracy, its wealth and culture," the county seat of which, Natchez, impressed the passing
visitor, even after the desolation of war, as an abode of luxury and
refinement. . . .

5. James Ford Rhodes, *History of the United States from the Compromise of
1850* (New York, 1906), VI, 156–57, 159, 206–7, 213, 232–35.

The new governor [Adelbert Ames] sincerely endeavored to carry out the Reconstruction Acts in the letter and spirit. He believed that, since the negroes were in the majority, their was the right to rule; and he constituted himself their champion, convinced as he was that the white people when in power would override them and deprive them of the right to vote. Nevertheless he overrated their mental capacity and their moral caliber. Like the men who had enacted Congressional reconstruction, he did not appreciate the great fact of race, that between none of the important races of mankind was there a difference so wide as between the Caucasian and the Negro. . . .

Even worse than that of Louisiana and Mississippi was the suffering of South Carolina. Worse indeed than the desolation of the war was that of the negro-carpet-bag rule from 1868 to 1874. And universal negro suffrage had a fair trial. The number of coloured men of the age of twenty-one and upward was 85,475 as against 62,547 white. With rare exceptions the negroes could vote freely and fearlessly and it is undoubted that, at every election until 1876, the coloured men who went to the polls far outnumbered the whites. . . . All the coloured men were Republicans. . . . As the negroes came to realize that they furnished practically all the votes of the Republican party they demanded a larger share of the offices and, as a result of the election of 1872, there was a coloured Lieutenant-Governor, Treasurer and other State officials, President of the Senate and Speaker, Clerk and Chairman of the Ways and Means Committee of the House.

Into such hands had the government of South Carolina fallen. Though an oligarchy before the war, it had been economical, pure, honest and dignified. Able men had sat in the governor's chair; the legislature was a creditable body. A prime requisite for any office in the State was integrity. And now for six years bribery, corruption and dishonesty ran riot. . . .

Given character and fitness as the proper tests for candidates for office, the negroes almost always voted wrong. . . .

No large policy in our country has ever been so conspicuous a failure as that of forcing universal negro suffrage upon the South. The negroes who simply acted out their nature were not to blame. How indeed could they have acquired political honesty? What idea could barbarism thrust into slavery obtain of the rights of property? Even among the Aryans of education and intelligence public integrity has been a plant of slow growth. From the days of the Grecian and Roman republics to our own, men have stolen from the State who would defraud no individual. With his crude ideas of honesty between man and man, what could have been expected of the negro when he got his hand in the public till? The scheme of Reconstruction pandered to the ignorant negroes, the knavish white natives and the vulturous adventurers who flocked from the North; and these neutralized the work of honest Republicans who were officers of State. Intelligence and property stood bound and helpless under negro-carpet-bag rule. . . .

From the Republican policy came no real good to the negroes. Most of them developed no political capacity, and the few who raised themselves above the mass did not reach a high order of intelligence. At different periods two served in the United States Senate, twenty in the House; they left no mark on the legislation of their time; none of them, in comparison with their white associates, attained the least distinction. . . .

# 15

# Black Writers Begin a Reassessment

*Black writers led the way in reassessing the role of black Reconstructionists and dispelling the legend perpetuated and given respectability by historians like Fleming and Rhodes. In 1905, the same year Fleming's book on Alabama was published,* The Aftermath of Slavery: A Study of the Condition and Environment of the American Negro, *by William A. Sinclair, appeared. Sinclair, who had lived in South Carolina during Reconstruction, revived an interpretation similar to that of Wendell Phillips and the other abolitionists. Booker T. Washington, who usually deprecated political activity by Negroes, felt that Radical Reconstruction had been a mistake. Nevertheless, he recognized that Reconstruction had produced a remarkable group of black political leaders, as the selection from his* Story of the Negro *shows.*

*Far more important in bringing about new research as well as a re-evaluation of the Reconstruction era was the work of W. E. B. Du Bois. At the meeting of the American Historical Association in 1909, he read "Reconstruction and Its Benefits," a paper expanding and supporting some of Sinclair's assertions about the constructive achievements of black Reconstructionists. In the last selection in this section, Horace Mann Bond asks to what extent black Reconstructionists represented the aspirations of the black masses.*

### WILLIAM A. SINCLAIR [6]

These Northern men who had settled in the South, and . . . the loyalists of the South responded to the call to assist in reconstructing the Southern states, because they rejoiced that the day of judgment had come to the South, and with their help Old Glory would flutter over a restored Union.

And the colored people! They bubbled over with rejoicings;

6. William A. Sinclair, *The Aftermath of Slavery: A Study of the Condition and Environment of the American Negro* (Boston, 1905), pp. 90–91, 102–3.

there was nothing that they would not have done for "the Lincoln government" and to sustain the North. There was not a colored man in the South who would not have borne arms in defence of the nation. If the South had tried "guerilla warfare" after General Lee's surrender, then the very last guerilla would have been driven to cover simply by arming the 700,000 colored men.

These three classes rendered the nation services of inestimable value in a most critical and perilous hour,—services for which the nation owes a lasting and incalculable debt of gratitude. There has been entirely too much random abuse of "carpet-baggers" and "scalawags." It is time to call a halt to these indiscriminate denunciations. . . . The white people of the South themselves are responsible for the so-called negro domination and carpet-bag governments. They threw away two opportunities to reconstruct, and for a third time refused even to share in the work of reconstruction. If some stealing and plundering accompanied the performance, theirs was the blame. . . . And with reference to negro suffrage, it is all-important to consider the fundamental truths connected therewith.

The giving of the ballot to the negro became the necessary means for the accomplishment of the rehabilitation of the Southern states; and the use of the ballot in the hands of the negro was effective in achieving the following results:

First: It established the sovereignty of the nation.

Second: It utterly destroyed all that was vicious, mischievous, and menacing in the doctrines of state rights.

Third: It made effective the Thirteenth Amendment, and enacted the Fourteenth and Fifteenth Amendments to the Constitution of the United States—giving rise to the strange paradox, unique in the history of the world, that the ballot of the ex-slave had become necessary to save the face of a conquering nation, preserve the fruits of victory, and assist in the enactment of laws which made his own freedom secure; and it wrote his own citizenship ineffaceably into the Constitution, the organic law of the land.

Fourth: It was effective in causing the adoption of free constitutions for the Southern states, the establishment of orderly government in them, and, in a word, rehabilitating them and restoring them to practical and proper relations with the Union.

Fifth: It gave the South its first system of Free Public Schools, a benefaction and blessing of incalculable value.

It is not, therefore, too much to say that the glory and the power of the republic to-day—the foremost and most powerful nation in the world—may be traced to the effective use of the negro as a soldier and as a voter in the most stormy and perilous hour of its existence. He was unquestionably the deciding factor. . . .

It must, therefore, appear evident to every serious, patriotic American who has more regard for liberty and Union than for race hatred and caste prejudice, that the bestowal of the ballot on the colored people, under the circumstances, and at the time, and in the manner that it was bestowed, was not only not a crime, but, on the contrary, was perhaps the sublimest act of enlightened statesmanship. . . .

### BOOKER T. WASHINGTON [7]

One of the results of the organisation of the Freedmen's Bureau was to give employment to a large number of ambitious colored men, and many representatives of the Negro race, who afterwards became prominent in politics, gained their first training in this direction as agents of the Freedmen's Bureau. . . .

It was unfortunate that the Freedmen's Bureau did not succeed in gaining the sympathy and support of the Southern people [i.e. whites]. This was the more unfortunate because, during the four years of its existence, the Freedmen had learned to look to this Bureau and its representatives for leading support and protection. The whole South has suffered from the fact that the former slaves were first introduced into political life as the opponents, instead of the political supporters, of their former masters. No part of the South has suffered more on this account, however, than the Negroes themselves. I do not mean to say that this rupture could have been avoided. It was one of the unfortunate consequences of the manner in which slavery was brought to an end in the Southern states.

In the early days of their freedom, in spite of the rather harsh legislation certain of the Southern legislatures [Black Codes], the temper of the Southern Freedmen was conciliatory. . . .

Among the Negroes of the Northern states who had gotten their political education under the Northern abolitionists, the trend of

7. Booker T. Washington, *Story of the Negro, 2 vols.* (New York, 1909), II, 10, 13–14, 19, 22–24, 28, 193.

sentiment was naturally much more radical than in the Southern states. . . .

Negroes sent two hundred and seven delegates out of eight hundred and thirty-four to the constitutional conventions which met, in 1867 and 1868. . . .

One of the surprising results of the Reconstruction Period was that there should spring from among the members of a race that had been held so long in slavery, so large a number of shrewd, resolute, resourceful, and even brilliant men, who became, during this brief period of storm and stress, the political leaders of the newly enfranchised race. Among them were sons of white planters by coloured mothers, like John M. Langston, P. S. B. Pinchback, and Josiah T. Settle [of Mississippi] who had given their children the advantages of an education in the Northern states. . . .

*There follows a sketch of some of the other leaders. Washington characterizes Elliott as a "most brilliant" and "unfortunate" leader.*

In considering the relation of the Negro people to this period it should be remembered that, outside of a few leaders, Negroes had very little influence upon the course of events. It was, to a very large extent, a white man's quarrel, and the Negro was the tennis ball which was batted backward and forward by the opposing parties. . . .

The fact is, that the coloured people, who went into politics directly after the war were, in most cases, what may be called the aristocracy of the race. Many of them had been practically, if not always legally, free, made so by their masters, who were at the same time their fathers, by whom they had been educated and from whom they frequently inherited considerable property. They had formed their lives and characters on the models of the aristocratic Southern people, among whom they were raised, and they believed that politics was the only sort of activity that was fit for a gentleman to engage in. The conditions which existed directly after the war offered these men the opportunity to step in and make themselves the political leaders of the masses of people.

### W. E. B. DU BOIS [8]

There is danger to-day that between the intense feeling of the South and the conciliatory spirit of the North grave injustice will be done to the negro American in the history of Reconstruction. Those who see in negro suffrage the cause of the main evils of Reconstruction must remember that if there had not been a single freedman left in the South after the war the problems of Reconstruction would still have been grave. . . .

Granted then that the negroes were to some extent venal but to a much larger extent ignorant and deceived, the question is: did they show any signs of a disposition to learn better things? The theory of democratic government is not that the will of the people is always right, but rather that normal human beings of average intelligence will, if given a chance, learn the right and best course by bitter experience. This is precisely what the negro voters showed indubitable signs of doing. First they strove for schools to abolish ignorance, and, second, a large and growing number of them revolted against the carnival of extravagance and stealing that marred the beginning of Reconstruction, and joined with the best elements to institute reform; and the greatest stigma on the white South is not that it opposed negro suffrage and resented theft and incompetence, but that when it saw the reform movement growing and even in some cases triumphing, and a larger and larger number of black voters learning to vote for honesty and ability, it still preferred a Reign of Terror to a campaign of education, and disfranchised negroes instead of punishing rascals. . . . But unfortunately there was one thing that the white South feared more than negro dishonesty, ignorance, and incompetency, and that was negro honesty, knowledge, and efficiency.

In the midst of all these difficulties the negro governments in the South accomplished much of positive good. We may recognize three things which negro rule gave to the South:

1. Democratic government.
2. Free public schools.
3. New social legislation.

8. W. E. B. Du Bois, "Reconstruction and Its Benefits," *American Historical Review* 15 (July, 1910), 781, 792–93, 795–99.

Two states will illustrate conditions of government in the South before and after negro rule. In South Carolina there was before the war a property qualification for office-holders, and, in part, for voters. The Constitution of 1868, on the other hand, was a modern democratic document. . . . It especially took up new subjects of social legislation, declaring navigable rivers free public highways, instituting homestead exemptions, establishing boards of county commissioners, providing for a new penal code of laws, establishing universal manhood suffrage "without distinction of race or color," devoting six sections to charitable and penal institutions and six to corporations, providing separate property for married women, etc. Above all, eleven sections of the Tenth Article were devoted to the establishment of a complete public-school system.

So satisfactory was the constitution thus adopted by negro suffrage and by a convention composed of a majority of blacks that the state lived twenty-seven years under it without essential change and when the constitution was revised in 1895, the revision was practically nothing more than an amplification of the Constitution of 1868. No essential advance step of the former document was changed except the suffrage article.

In Mississippi the Constitution of 1868 was, as compared with that before the war, more democratic. . . . This democracy brought forward new leaders and men and definitely overthrew the old Southern aristocracy. Among these new men were negroes of worth and ability. John R. Lynch when speaker of the Mississippi house of representatives was given a public testimonial by Republicans and Democrats. . . .

*Du Bois also mentions Francis L. Cardozo of South Carolina and Jonathan C. Gibbs of Florida.*

There is no doubt but that the thirst of the black man for knowledge—a thirst which has been too persistent and durable to be mere curiosity or whim—gave birth to the public free-school system of the South. It was the question upon which black voters and legislators insisted more than anything else and while it is possible to find some vestiges of free schools in some of the Southern States before the war yet a universal, well-established system dates from the day that the black man got political power. . . .

We are apt to forget that in all human probability the granting of negro manhood suffrage and the passage of the Fifteenth Amendment were decisive in rendering permanent the foundation of the negro common school. . . .

Finally, in legislation covering property, the wider functions of the state, the punishment of crime and the like, it is sufficient to say that the laws on these points established by Reconstruction legislatures were not only different from and even revolutionary to the laws in the older South, but they were so wise and so well suited to the needs of the new South that in spite of a retrogressive movement following the overthrow of the negro governments the mass of this legislation, with elaboration and development, still stands on the statute books of the South. . . . Practically the whole new growth of the South has been accomplished under laws which black men helped to frame thirty years ago. I know of no greater compliment to negro suffrage.

### HORACE MANN BOND [9]

*The Negroes.* The role of the Negro during Reconstruction has been given as many different interpretations as there are theories of racial psychology. No esoteric explanation of their behaviour is needed in this essay; it may be helpful to remember that the Negroes were ex-slaves, and we know what the institution of chattel slavery consciously designed to produce as its labor force. That the masses were ignorant goes without saying; that they were disorganized and restless was inevitable.

And yet these masses—these ignorant and restless ex-slaves— knew exactly what they needed. Their slogan has been ridiculed for nearly seventy years, and probably will be so for eternity. What they asked of the Government which had set them free was, indeed, a monstrosity. They asked for a subsistence farmstead—for forty acres and a mule.

The leadership of this mass of ignorance was more important

9. Horace Mann Bond, "Social and Economic Forces in Alabama Reconstruction," *Journal of Negro History* 23 (July, 1938), pp. 296–97. Copyright © 1938 by The Association for the Study of Negro Life and History, Inc. Reprinted by permission of the publisher.

than the mass itself in directing its energies. This leadership has been alternately blamed and praised by partisans. Unfortunately, they left no documents which would help us understand what kind of men they were. We do know that they were frequently persons with an education equal or superior to that of the white politicians of their day, and that they had the same economic point of view. . . .

James T. Rapier was a mulatto of planting antecedents, a well-educated man with a cultural background probably unsurpassed in Alabama among his contemporaries, whether white or black.

A significant fact about the Negro leadership prevalent during Alabama Reconstruction is that few were actually identified, in economic position, with the great mass of landless, utterly penniless Negro ex-slaves whom they purported to represent. The economic ambitions of the Negro leaders are reflected in Rapier's self-conscious pride in the ownership of a large plantation in North Alabama. The Negro leaders of a "radical" party had little reason to advocate the economic radicalism of Agrarian Republicanism. They were bent on achieving, within the economic framework which favored them, the social and political privileges which were the dower of the white Conservatives whom they publicly opposed. . . .

# 16
## Some Recent Interpretations

### LOUISIANA: OSCAR JAMES DUNN

*In the following article, A. E. Perkins evaluates the career of Oscar James Dunn, a former slave and the first black to be elected to a state administrative post.*[10]

Oscar James Dunn, Lieutenant Governor of Louisiana from 1868 to 1871, was, in character, vision, prudence and foresight an unusual man. In spite of the handicaps of slavery and a slave society, he lifted himself, even before the Civil War, to a status of note and respectability. . . .

It is more than probable that he was born in 1820 or 1821, and that at the time of his death he was fifty or fifty-one years old. Information about Dunn's relations, bilateral or lineal, are [*sic*] meager. Nothing is known of his parents. . . .

Dunn received no formal education, and whatever training he had was probably gotten largely after he was grown and had emancipated himself. His language and bearing indicated that he had secured a good fundamental education. He was in all probability a good student for he had been, after becoming an efficient plasterer, a popular instructor in violin music. Where, from whom, and when he received his education is not known, nor how he secured his knowledge and skill of the violin. But we must assume that it was largely between 1845 and 1860, for prior to that time he had been a slave and had shown disappointment at his plight by running away. He had probably done little self-improvement before that time. . . .

His addresses reflect culture and education which could have been, of course, largely his secretary's composition. But the clear expression and guarded, dignified restraint were very evidently Dunn's. Only a few of Dunn's addresses are recorded. He in fact

10. A. E. Perkins, "Oscar James Dunn," *Phylon* 4, no. 2 (Second quarter, 1943), pp. 105–8, 110–11, 113, 115–17, 121. Copyright © 1943 by Butler University. Reprinted by permission of the publisher.

made but few speeches. He seems to have been a man of action rather than of words. . . .

Dunn had been made captain in the Union Army of New Orleans and the Gulf under General Benjamin F. Butler. Notwithstanding his resignation from the army as captain "in resentment for the promotion of an inferior white man over him," he yet held the high regard of military and civil leaders. General Phil H. Sheridan, commander of the Army of the Fifth Military District composed of Louisiana and Texas, appointed him a member of the Junior City Council of New Orleans.

On August 6, 1866, Dunn took his seat in the Junior Commission Council. In his activity as a member of this body he exhibited a clear vision of the city's civic needs. . . . During his two years as a member of the Junior Council and in joint meetings with the Common Council he spoke, made motions and introduced resolutions not confined wholly to racial matters. . . .

*The author gives an account of the nomination and election of Henry Clay Warmoth, the white carpetbagger, for the position of governor and of Dunn as lieutenant governor in 1868.*

Through a rapid series of clever political maneuvers Warmouth had become head of one of the American commonwealths. One of his close associates was the colored leader, P. B. S. Pinchback, later himself governor of Louisiana for a short period. It is certain that he knew Pinchback more intimately than Dunn, for Pinchback had gained Warmoth's attention through his able leadership evident in the Constitutional Convention. Indeed, he became Warmoth's "first man" and aristocrats and millionaires waited in ante-rooms while this shrewd and adventurous politican sat with the governor behind closed doors making and unmaking laws and men. They were both men of reckless ambitions and of questionable political morals. If we followed out their public careers, we would find them finally at daggers points.

It logically followed too, that Warmoth and Dunn would break. Dunn had aspirations and the party's support. Warmoth had ambitions and a well "greased" machine. Pinchback was not a whit less ambitious nor less shrewd and audacious than Warmoth. These three able leaders were all but sure to move at counter aims somewhere as events matured and issues ripened. With three men looking at one office, a United States senatorship, two had to miss it. Dunn had the lead on the other two aspirants. He had President Grant's ear.

Warmoth and Pinchback were looked upon as interlopers, the one from Illinois and the other from Ohio. Dunn was a native and well-known; he knew local feelings and sentiment. He was regarded, too, as a straightforward dependable man. No critic, even rabid Southerners, ever pointed to any graft, misappropriation or illicit public practice by him. . . .

The chasm between Lieutenant-Governor Dunn and the Warmoth-Pinchback clique widened, . . . In the spring of 1871, Governor Warmoth suffered an accident to his right foot and went across the lake to Pass Christian, Mississippi, for recuperation. By the Constitution, Dunn became governor as much as if Warmoth had died or resigned or was in Europe. But Warmoth wanted to deny this constitutional right. . . .

An acute situation arose between the Governor and Lieutenant-Governor Dunn. The Republican State Convention assembled in New Orleans August 9, 1870, for the purpose of nominating a ticket and appointing a State Central Committee. Both the Governor and the Lieutenant-Governor were present as delegates; both were nominated to preside. ". . . here the Governor met his first check; he was defeated by his Negro subordinate." . . .

The rupture between Lieutenant-Governor Dunn and Governor Henry Clay Warmoth was fatal and far-reaching. It marked definitely the beginning of the downfall of the Republican party in Louisiana, and served as a wedge to split it, thus permitting the Democratic Party to enter its ranks. Had the Republicans held together at this time they might have been a bulwark in the presidential contest of 1876.

Dunn severely arraigned Warmoth in a letter to Horace Greeley:

> . . . There are 90,000 voters in the State, . . . 84,000 of whom are coloured . . . Nineteen-twentieths of the Republican Party . . . are opposed to the present State Executive. . . .
>
> In all candor, we believe that his Excellency, Governor H. C. Warmoth, is officially derelict and politically untrustworthy. . . .

> We cannot and will not support him, even though the New York *Tribune* should remain his champion, for such support would inevitably involve the disastrous defeat of the Republican party in the State of Louisiana.

Now by Dunn's capture of the Republican State Convention, he had within his grasp the forces to elevate him to the governorship, and if events ran true to form, finally to a United States senatorship. . . . Furthermore, this new leadership by Dunn meant nothing less than Warmoth's being shoved into the background, or mayhap his complete political elimination. It too was an ill omen for Pinchback, who now with his natural dexterity began a measured retreat from Warmoth's camp. It followed, however, since Dunn's light was pushing Pinchback into the shadows that he and Warmoth might get together against Dunn. It cannot be said that Pinchback cared much for Dunn. They were very different in habits, temperament and character.

Pinchback and Warmoth had never really trusted each other. "I practically appointed Pinchback lieutenant-governor of the State, and he came nearly to wrecking me," says Warmoth.

Warmoth had his defeated faction withdrawn from the State Republican Convention of which Dunn had secured the presidency and the majority of the delegates' votes and support, and formed a "rump" convention, disapproved by President Grant and most of the Republican State officials. Pinchback was made chairman of the revolting convention, and Warmoth had staged a dramatic demonstration by riding with him down Canal Street in his liveried coach while hired spectators wildly applauded and trained lackeys unleashed his span and drew the carriage in wild gusto through crowded streets.

The Dunn convention, recognized generally as the legal one by federal officials and authorities, read Warmoth out of the party, censured his official organ, the *Republican,* pledged an amendment limiting the state debt, advocated public schools. Warmoth, the wily politician, thus found himself circumvented, beaten by his "Negro subordinate," finally deserted by his ally Pinchback, and "double-crossed" by the Democrats to whom he had lately fled for succor. They embraced him, deserted him, and left him. . . .

*Dunn died suddenly on November 22, 1871. There were*
*rumors that he had been poisoned.*

It is probable that his death changed the course of Negro history. Had he lived he would have in all probability held Louisiana in
the Republican column in 1876. Hayes would have had no need to
sell the race to the South by withdrawing civil protection from it in
order to be president. He could have been president with no cloud
on the title, if Louisiana had stayed definitely in the Republican
column. . . .

There is found no adverse criticism on Oscar J. Dunn among
white or black, either before or since his death. The [New Orleans]
*Times* carried notices of respect on his death from practically every
public institution in New Orleans. . . .

It may be easily seen then, why no Southern critic of the politics
of the times ever makes any comment on Dunn. He is merely mentioned and passed over. A revelation of his clear inside political
life would prove too much against the establishment of anti-Negro
political propaganda. It definitely refutes the general Southern
attitude that all Negro politicians were crooks, thieves, ignoramuses,
and public plunderers.

### SOUTH CAROLINA: JONATHAN JASPER WRIGHT, FRANCIS L. CARDOZO, AND ROBERT SMALLS

*The selections following deal with the careers of three*
*of the leading black Reconstructionists in South Carolina.*
*The sketch of Jonathan Jasper Wright, the only black mem-*
*ber of a state supreme court, is by Robert H. Woody, co-*
*author with Francis B. Simkins of* South Carolina During
Reconstruction *(1932), which was probably more influential*
*than any other single book in leading scholars to reappraise*
*the Reconstruction era in the South. The second selection, by*
*Edwin F. Sweat, is from an article portraying Francis L.*
*Cardozo, who was successively secretary of state and state*
*treasurer. Although there were attempts to impeach both of*
*them, Wright and Cardozo were moderates, generally re-*
*spected by whites as able and incorruptible. The third selec-*
*tion is an evaluation of the career of congressman Robert*

*Smalls, the "king of Beaufort," taken from the recent biography by Okon Edet Uya.*

### Jonathan Jasper Wright[11]

Jonathan Jasper Wright is a unique character in the annals of Negro history, for he is the only member of the race who ever sat on the bench of the Supreme Court of any American state; it is this distinction which gives him a place in history. . . .

Like the majority of Negroes who became prominent in the South during Reconstruction, Wright was a carpet-bagger, a native of Pennsylvania who had been educated in New York and who had acquired an education superior to any obtainable by the Southern Negro. . . .

Perhaps it was his teaching experience and legal training which induced the American Missionary Society to send Wright, along with others, to South Carolina in 1865 to organize Negro schools. He was stationed at Beaufort in the very center of the State's Negro population. After remaining one year in Beaufort, he returned to Pennsylvania; there he achieved the distinction of being the first Negro to pass the tests of the legal examiners of his county and be admitted to practice law in Pennsylvania. He had been refused a legal examination in 1865, but after the passage of the first Civil Rights Bill over Johnson's veto, he was given an examination and was admitted to the bar on August 13, 1866. The same year Wright returned to Beaufort with an appointment from General O. O. Howard as legal advisor of refugees and freedmen. . . .

Wright was elected a member of the constitutional convention of South Carolina. . . . He was chosen one of the five vice-presidents of the convention, he and William Beverly Nash being the two colored vice-presidents. Wright spoke frequently but usually to the point; he showed much good sense, and he exerted a moderating and restraining influence upon the more radical colored members of the convention. . . .

Following the constitutional convention, Wright was elected a State senator from Beaufort. In the senate he immediately assumed

11. Robert H. Woody, "Jonathan Jasper Wright, Associate Justice of the Supreme Court of South Carolina, 1870–1877," *Journal of Negro History* 18 (April, 1933), pp. 114–22, 130–31. Copyright © 1933 by The Association for the Study of Negro Life and History, Inc. Reprinted by permission of the publisher.

a commanding position. He had the reputation of being the ablest colored man in the State, and he even won the respect of some of his Democratic contemporaries. . . .

Wright's personal appearance was somewhat striking. He was a full-blooded Negro, nearly six feet tall, with a somewhat long, narrow head, and a rather high, protuberant forehead. . . . Colonel A. K. McClure, in writing sketches of members of the legislature for the New York *Tribune,* said Wright was the most notable Negro in that body, "with a finely chiseled face and handsomely developed head." He was nearly always good-humored, although when speaking he was serious rather than facetious. He was inclined to lisp in his speech, so he spoke in a slow, precise tone, and in rather grandiloquent language. . . .

There seems to have been a definite intention on the part of the Republican legislature to elect a colored man to succeed [S. L.] Hoge [as a member of the supreme court]. . . . R. H. "Daddy" Cain, Negro legislator and preacher usually found on the side of reform, nominated Wright. With few exceptions the small Democratic minority in the legislature voted for Wright. . . .

It is curious to note the public reaction to Wright's election. There was not that torrent of abuse which the press usually poured out upon scalawags and Negroes who were elected to high office. . . . The explanation seems to be that the press and the people generally recognized the proven good character of Wright, and while they did not approve of the election of a Negro to the Supreme Court, they were perfectly aware of the fact that the legislature had acted with much moderation and good sense in electing Wright other than some less fit person. . . .

. . . Wright's career on the bench evidenced considerable ability. While it is true that all the important cases involving novel points of law or large political or economic interests were decided by [Franklin J.] Moses [Sr.] or [A. J.] Willard, of the 425 cases decided during his seven-year tenure, eighty-seven were written by Wright. He dissented in only one case. His written opinions were clearly expressed and judicious in tone. They involved no intricate legal points, and it is probably true that Wright had no ambition to shine as a great jurist. He seems to have willingly permitted his colleagues to assume the more important cases. As far as is known, no serious friction ever developed between Wright and his two white colleagues. It is true, also, that he never made himself obnoxious in a political way by leaving the bench to take the stump. He seems to have been assiduous in attention to his duties and to have performed them creditably. . . .

It should be emphasized that Wright was a moderate in politics, seeking to conciliate rather than to antagonize. At the same time he did not wish to reach a compromise by sacrificing the rights of his race. For example, in 1871 he brought a damage suit against the Richmond and Danville Railroad for having ejected him from a first-class white passenger car. The damages were claimed because he had been ejected from the car solely on account of color, notwithstanding that he held a first-class ticket. He recovered $1,200. In a speech in Charleston in 1872, Wright pointed out that all hopes of the Negro race for relief lay with the Federal Government. . . . [But] Wright concluded with the peroration:

Let us "envy not the oppressor . . ." nor cherish any malice or hatred in our hearts against any man because he has been a slaveholder, or because he differs with us in politics. Let us labor for the peace, union and prosperity of all our fellow-citizens of whatever race or color. . . .

## Francis L. Cardozo[12]

A brief examination of the public career of one trained, articulate, and incorruptible Negro who served in the government of his native state of South Carolina should prove revealing. . . . Such an individual was Francis L. Cardoza, a Negro born in the city of Charleston, South Carolina, February 1, 1837, of free parents.

This talented individual began his education in an antebellum school for Negroes in Charleston. He completed his formal training abroad, pursuing courses with distinction at the University of Glasgow, and rounding out his education with three years of formal training for the ministry at Presbyterian seminaries located in Edinburgh and London. From 1864 to 1865 he pastored in New Haven, Connecticut, leaving in the latter year to return to his native city where, on two separate occasions, he organized and successfully administered schools for the freedmen of the city.

12. Edward F. Sweat, "Francis L. Cardoza: Profile of Integrity in Reconstruction Politics," *ibid.* 46 (1961), 218–19, 223–25, 228–30, 232. Copyright © 1961 by The Association for the Study of Negro Life and History, Inc. Reprinted by permission of the publisher. Although Sweat uses the spelling "Cardoza," "Cardozo" appears to be the correct spelling.

His abiding faith in the efficacy of education and the democratic process shaped his life's work and determined his fate. To a large degree this explains why he devoted his energies to political and educational institutions rather than to the church. His election as a delegate to the South Carolina Constitutional Convention of 1868 marked the beginning of a comparatively brief, sometimes stormy, but distinguished political career. . . .

Just prior to the adjournment of the convention the Republican Party of the state assembled to nominate state officials and Congressmen. Cardoza was the party's choice for Secretary of State. . . . As the first such official under the new constitution he discharged the routine duties of the office. The most significant accomplishment during his term as Secretary of State was connected with the disposal of public lands in the state. . . . Cardoza, who actively campaigned for the Republican ticket, was closely allied with the Union League and served as president of the state council in 1870. In an address to the Grand Council, composed of the various councils of the state, he described the opposing party as a "strange combination of contradiction, inconsistency, and deception." He accepted the challenge of the opposition party to compare records, principles, and men, admitting that "the Republicans had made some mistakes which were almost unavoidable under the peculiar circumstances surrounding us," but he proposed to prove that "the many and substantial advantages which our short administration of a little more than two years has obtained for the state," entitled them "to the thanks and endorsement of the people, without regard to race, color, or previous condition."

On Wednesday, October 19, the election was held without any serious trouble, with the Republicans winning 85,071 to 51,537 for their opponents [Cardozo being elected state treasurer.] . . .

In his report for the fiscal year ending October 31, 1874, Cardoza showed the amount of bonds and stocks funded into consolidated bonds. . . . He estimated that up to that date the state had been saved the payment of nearly one million dollars worth of bonds and interest thereon at six percent for twenty years. . . .

Governor Chamberlain praised the report as a "luminous and complete exhibit of the operations of that department," . . . The *News and Courier* felt that "only knowledge of Governor Chamberlain's strength in and out of the state prevented the chagrined corruptionists from framing articles of impeachment against him."

The paper warned, however, that the wrath of these who would despoil the treasury was transferred to Treasurer Cardoza, who had been zealous in cooperating with the efforts at reform. That this was not idle fancy on the part of a newspaper was borne out when a special joint finance committee was called into existence and in due course made its report.

Once again the beleaguered Treasurer found himself the target of an investigating group. . . .

On March 10, the general assembly by the required majority in each house voted the address demanding Cardoza's removal from office. Despite Governor Chamberlain's bitter opposition the charges were argued before a joint session and were then debated by the two Houses. Cardoza was acquitted by votes of 63 to 45 and 19 to 11 in the lower House and Senate respectively. This victory was hailed by the Columbia *Union Herald* as a "triumph for official integrity, public duty, economy in expenditures, competency in offices and low taxes." . . .

Cardoza died in Washington on July 22, 1903. He had had a passion for economy in government in an age permeated by extravagance and incompetence, not alone in South Carolina and not peculiar to the Negro, but on a national scale and associated with men of all races. Present day opinion all too often inclines to the view that the presence of Negroes in Reconstruction governments represented the bizarre and absurd. . . . The political career of this native of South Carolina stands in sharp contrast to this estimate for the very reason that he brought into public life an intelligence, a vibrant sincerity, and a vigilance in guarding public funds that challenged the morality of the age. . . .

### Robert Smalls[13]

On February 26, 1915, the citizens of Beaufort and many prominent blacks gathered in the First Avenue Baptist Church where Smalls himself had worshiped for more than ten years. This time they had not come to listen to Smalls' "fine story" about the *Planter* or his political campaigns, or to honor him with cheers and pledges of support. Now they could honor him only with their tears. The

13. Okon Edet Uya, *From Slavery to Public Service: Robert Smalls, 1839–1915* (London: Oxford University Press, 1971), pp. 162–66. Copyright © 1971 by Oxford University Press, Inc. Reprinted by permission of the publisher.

Allen's Brass Band which had always accompanied him on political campaigns was there, but this time it played the solemn funeral march. Dr. Bythe Wood, a Beaufort minister, reminded the weeping crowd that they were there to pay the last respects to "a great citizen." Reverend P. P. Watson of Orangeburg added that the deceased was "one of the greatest Negroes." Dr. Coit, presiding elder of the African Methodist Episcopal Church for Beaufort, catalogued the "many beneficial legislative enactments attributed to the fertile brain of the general." After an impressive service and a Masonic ceremony, Robert Smalls was buried in the A.M.E. Churchyard on Craven Street. Very appropriately, the choir sang "Shall we meet beyond the river!" The funeral was "the largest ever held in this city and the floral offerings were numerous and beautiful," commented the Savannah *Tribune* on this last respect paid to a great black man and an authentic American hero. . . .

Daring, cool-headed, keen of mind, courageous, and firm on the principle of the equality of all men without regard to race and color, Robert Smalls was an outstanding leader of the Reconstruction decades and after.

Throughout his politically active years, Robert Smalls thought of himself not only as representing black people but as being black himself. He was not ashamed of his race and never lost an opportunity to remind whites of this fact. He was emphatic on the point that he was only one among his fellow blacks and insisted that his colleagues, black and white, see him as such. Smalls understood that blacks were discriminated against as a people and that the individual black person who did achieve "exceptional" status was really no freer from discrimination.

Except for the brief period in 1862, when the *Planter* episode brought him into national prominence, Robert Smalls never won the national plaudits showered on either Booker T. Washington or W. E. B. Du Bois. Though he maintained constant contact with Republican national administrations during his politically active years and profited from the spoils of office, thus functioning partly as an "out-group based leader," Smalls was essentially an "ethnic" leader with firm roots in his community. In a community that had no clearly defined upper or political class, Smalls, together with a few other individuals, came to symbolize the aspirations of the Beaufort blacks. He affected the patterns of behavior of his constituents, and wielded enormous power within his community, mainly because of his leadership qualities and because he delivered something more tangible than the rhetoric of racial unity and hope of improvement in terms of the educational and economic projects he promoted. If successful leadership can be judged by an ability to instill among the following a certain high degree of morale and an effectiveness in securing community goals, Smalls was certainly an effective leader of the Beaufort blacks in these years. . . .

Smalls did not, publicly or privately, show any respect for the system of race prejudice, and did not regard political or civil rights as a luxury, but as fundamental to the acquisition of the other needs of black people. He realized that political power was necessary for any economic gains, as is illustrated by his constant effort to use his political connections to secure economic benefits for his community. "The battle of life" for which Robert Smalls asked that black people be given "an equal chance" was an economic as well as a political one.

Since he accepted the political system of his day as a viable vehicle for effecting change and thereby eliminating the discrimination to which blacks were subjected, Smalls' political stance was essentially one of protest as opposed to any sort of revolution. To protest within the system meant that Smalls, as well as many of his black contemporaries, had to appeal to white sympathy, sense of decency, and fairness. The theme of fairness or equal treatment runs through nearly all of Smalls' important speeches. When making appeals in behalf of black people, Smalls always called for a return to the ideals on which the nation was founded.

Like many of his contemporaries, Smalls saw integration as the goal of the black struggle and believed that the "inherent justice" of the American system of government as expressed in the Declaration of Independence would triumph over the forces that had conspired to make the country depart from its principles. Black people, in his thinking, because they possessed in abundance those "virtues which adorn the human race"—gentleness, patience, affection, and generosity—would play an important part in making the American dream come true. He firmly believed and constantly quoted the words of President Lincoln to the effect that "the ballot in the hands of the black man may serve in some trying hour to come to preserve the jewel of liberty to the diadem of the Republic." As for white people, he perceived the significance of Reconstruction policy as a white commitment to the goal of equality for all Americans, irrespective of their color. Using the advantages of hindsight, we know that Smalls' hope for integration, equal opportunity, and practical citizenship for black people proved unrealistic. Reality was the emergence of a color-caste system imbedded in the laws, behavior, and attitudes of white America. . . .

### MISSISSIPPI'S BLACK LEADERS

*The Negro in Mississippi, 1865–1890, by Vernon L. Wharton, published in 1947, is a pioneer work by a white scholar on the role of blacks in a southern state. The following selection deals with black leaders during the Reconstruction years.*[14]

The only place on the [Republican] ticket [of 1869] which went to a Negro was that for the office of secretary of state. This nominee, James D. Lynch, was the first man of his race to hold a major office in Mississippi, and was probably the most remarkable of the Negroes who rose to prominence during the period. An able and highly educated Pennsylvanian, he came to Mississippi in 1868 to take charge of the activities of the Methodist Episcopal Church in the state. Within three years, he had gained a place in the hearts of the Negroes that no other leader of either race has ever challenged. . . . A Democratic paper called him "the most popular carpet-bagger in the State—the best educated man, and the best speaker, and the most effective orator, of that party, in Mississippi; and, withal, as much of a gentleman as he can be with his present white associations." To John R. Lynch, one of his colleagues, he was "the Henry Ward Beecher of the colored race." Throughout his brief career of distinguished service to church and state, Lynch maintained the respect of his white opponents. In 1875, however, as a candidate for the Republican nomination for Congress, he was dragged into court by white Republican rivals on a charge of adultery. Deprived of the nomination, he died almost immediately. Negroes say that the cause was a broken heart. However true that

14. Vernon Lane Wharton, *The Negro in Mississippi, 1865–1890* (Chapel Hill, N. C.: University of North Carolina Press, 1947), pp. 154–55, 158–64. Copyright © 1947 by the University of North Carolina. Reprinted by permission of the publisher.

may be, Lynch was the most brilliant representative of his race ever to play a part in the affairs of the state, and his influence on the freedmen between 1869 and 1873 was greater than that of any other man. . . .

Mississippi was extremely fortunate in the character of her more important Negro Republican leaders. . . .

Hiram Rhodes Revels . . . was the first Negro to serve in the United States Senate, in which body he completed the unexpired term of Jefferson Davis. . . . During the war, after assisting in the organization of Negro regiments in Maryland and Missouri, he went to Mississippi, where he organized churches, lectured, and attempted to organize schools. An interlude of two years in Kansas and Missouri was followed by his return to Mississippi, where he settled in Natchez as presiding elder of the Methodist Episcopal Church. Immediately, and almost entirely against his will, he was drawn into politics.

After a term of service on the city council of Natchez, Revels was persuaded by John R. Lynch to enter the race for the state senate. His election to that body opened the way for his advancement to a much higher office. It had been agreed that the short term available in the United States Senate should go to a Negro. So impressive was the prayer with which Revels opened the proceedings of the upper house that he immediately became the candidate of the Negro legislators.

In Washington, Revels naturally attracted a great deal of attention. Tall, portly, dignified, and an excellent speaker, he delighted those who had worked for the elevation of his race, and to some extent eased the misgivings of those who had opposed it. His actual accomplishments as a new man in the short session of the Senate were few. None of the bills introduced by him was passed. He did, however, speak effectively on several occasions, and in his speaking and voting he showed intelligence and moderation. His support of a bill for the general removal of the political disabilities of Southern whites was especially effective. In his work outside the Senate, he succeeded in obtaining the admission of Negro mechanics to work in the United States Navy Yard.

Upon his return to Mississippi, Revels was appointed to the presidency of Alcorn University, the new state college for Negroes. . . . Essentially a timid man, more of a scholar than a leader, and anxiously desirous of peace, he came more and more to be dominated by white Democrats. . . . In spite of his extreme caution and timidity, Revels throughout his career was a credit to his race. Had there been more like him, both white and black, some compromise would have brought peace in Mississippi.

A much more prominent figure than Revels was Blanche Kelso Bruce, the only Negro ever to serve a full term in the United States Senate, and the man described by Benjamin Brawley as "probably the most astute political leader the Negro ever had." . . . To the end of his distinguished career, Bruce was always the gentleman, graceful, polished, self-assured, and never humble. He scorned the use of the phrase "colored man," often declaring "I am a negro, and proud of my race." . . .

Equally remarkable was the career of John R. Lynch. . . . After a brief term as a justice of the peace, he resigned to become, at the age of twenty-two, a member of the state legislature. There he made a remarkable impression. In spite of his youth, and in spite of the fact that there were only thirty-two Negroes in the House, he was elected speaker in 1872. Democrats and Republicans alike praised his ability and impartiality. In November, 1872, he was elected to Congress, and in December, 1873, he entered that body as its youngest member.

On the floor, Lynch showed himself to be perfectly at ease, making his first formal speech within eight days of the opening of the session. Of a distinctly aristocratic appearance, slender and active, with a very light complexion and regular features, he spoke fluently, tersely, and correctly. Franklin A. Montgomery wrote that he had few, if any, superiors as a stump speaker. His effective delivery and ready wit appealed to blacks and whites alike. Montgomery advised Democratic speakers to avoid clashing with him in debate. Serving in the Forty-Third, Forty-Fourth, and Forty-Seventh Congresses, he probably possessed as much influence at the White House as any Negro has ever had, being frequently called for consultation by Grant and Garfield. Throughout his public career, no scandal ever touched him, and by 1880 the Jackson *Clarion* was calling him "the ablest man of his race in the South."

Refusing offers from Lamar and Cleveland of appointments based on his retirement from politics, Lynch remained in the Republican party, serving as the temporary chairman of its national convention in 1884, and as fourth auditor of the treasury under Harrison. After studying and practicing law, he entered the army in 1898, and served until 1911, when he retired with the rank of major. He then opened law offices in Chicago, and became a power in the Republican organization in that city. In the meantime, he wrote three books on Reconstruction and his political experiences. . . .

Even more remarkable than the rise of Bruce, Lynch, and others to prominent positions in the state and nation was the amazingly rapid development of efficient local leaders among the Negroes. There is something fascinating about the suddenness with which, all over the state, they emerged from the anonymity of slavery to become directors and counselors for their race. In general, it can be said that they were not Negroes who had held positions of leadership under the old regime; the characteristics which made a man a slave driver or foreman were not those which would allow him to organize a Loyal League. Almost none of them came from the small group who had been free before the war. Such men, as barbers, artisans, or small farmers, had depended too long on the favor of the whites for the maintenance of their existence. Servility had become a part of them. Most of this group became Democrats, although a number of the younger element in the comparatively liberal region around Natchez gained prominence in the Republican organization.

A large portion of the minor Negro leaders were preachers, lawyers or teachers from the free states or from Canada. Their education and their independent attitude gained for them immediate favor and leadership. Of the natives who became their rivals the majority had been urban slaves, blacksmiths, carpenters, clerks, or waiters in hotels and boarding houses; a few of them had been favored body-servants of affluent whites. Most of them were more intelligent than the mass of their fellows and had picked up something of a smattering of education, at least to the point of being able to read and write. There was a general tendency for them to combine preaching with their politics; as Sir George Campbell has said, they were rather preachers because they were leaders than leaders because they were preachers. The death rate of these local organizers, both during and immediately after Reconstruction, was alarmingly high. . . .

### FLORIDA'S BLACK LEADERS

*The following selection, dealing with the black political leaders of Florida, is taken from Joe M. Richardson,* The Negro in the Reconstruction of Florida, *which was published in 1965.*[15]

Only one Negro from Florida, Congressman Josiah T. Walls, achieved national prominence during this period. Walls was born of free parents in Winchester, Virginia, on December 30, 1842. He learned the trade of a miller at which he was engaged until the outbreak of the Civil War. During the war Walls was pressed into a Confederate artillery battery as a servant. Captured by Union forces at the Battle of Yorktown in May, 1862, Walls went to Harrisburg, Pennsylvania, where he attended school for one year. In July, 1863, he enlisted in the Third Regiment of United State Colored Infantry as a private. He was present at the battle on St. Johns Island, and assisted in taking Fort Wagner. Upon the fall of Fort Wagner, Walls was sent to Jacksonville as a sergeant major and instructor of artillery. He was mustered out in Florida in November, 1865, and settled in Alachua County as a farmer. Walls was a "good farmer," a native white said in later years, and neighboring planters insisted he could get more and better work out of free labor than any man in the vicinity.

Walls first became involved in politics when he was sent as a delegate to the Republican Convention in Tallahassee in 1867. He was then sent as a delegate to the constitutional convention of 1868, where, according to available records, he played a minor role. Elected to the lower house of the State legislature in 1868, he remained for two sessions and in 1869 was elected to the senate from the Thirteenth District. While in the lower house he was probably the most active Negro on the floor, and he was one of the two or three most important representatives of his race in the senate. On the basis of the limited reports in the legislative jour-

15. Joe M. Richardson, *The Negro in the Reconstruction of Florida, 1865–1877* (Tallahassee, Fla.: Florida State University Press, 1965), pp. 177–79, 184–87, 189–90. Copyright © 1965 by Florida State University. Reprinted by permission of the publisher.

nals, Walls was not only active, but also quite capable of holding his own with the more experienced members. When a convention met in Gainesville in the summer of 1870 to nominate a congress-man, Walls was a natural choice for the Negroes who were deter-mined to have a man of their race.

By 1870 Walls was known and respected throughout the State. . . .

When Walls was first elected, he was the State's only member of the House of Representatives. Walls was not educated to deal with many of the important issues on the national scene, but did well under the circumstances. . . .

Walls was a "zealous advocate" of the interests of his state, and a Florida "booster." He encouraged settlers to move to Florida, claiming that " 'my own sunny state' " has "a thousand rare and valuable inducements to immigration. . . ." Of all Negro con-gressmen he was "perhaps the most persistent in the effort to secure improvement for his district and State." He introduced at least fifty-one bills, several of them for internal improvements in Florida. . . .

Walls was the only Florida Negro of national eminence, but there were several able Negro politicians in the State. One of the most capable men in Florida, white or Negro, was Jonathan C. Gibbs [an ordained Presbyterian minister, educated at Dartmouth College and Princeton Theological Seminary]. . . .

Gibbs was elected to the constitutional convention of 1868, and aligned with the radical faction of the Republican Party, though his speeches were usually temperate. He was one of the outstanding Negro members of the convention. . . . Later in the year [1868] Gibbs was appointed secretary of state after the first appointee, George J. Alden, a native white Unionist, joined the governor's enemies in an attempt to impeach him. The appointment of Gibbs undoubtedly strengthened [Governor Harrison] Reed's position with the freedmen, who believed the governor had neglected them. As secretary of state, Gibbs was a trusted public servant, and worked closely with Reed. In the governor's absence he served as chair-man pro tem of the Board of Commissioners of Public Institutions. He was Reed's right-hand man, and was respected by other cabinet officers.

Even Democrats commended Gibbs for his fairness. . . . Being fair did not shield Gibbs from the hatred of the Ku Klux Klan.

His brother visited him while he was secretary of state, and found him in a "well-appointed residence," but sleeping in the attic where he kept "considerable of an arsenal." Gibbs said he had slept in the attic for several months for better vantage as the Ku Klux had threatened his life.

When Governor Reed was succeeded in January, 1873, by Ossian B. Hart, Gibbs was appointed superintendent of public instruction. According to a Negro contemporary, the freedmen threatened to desert the Republican Party unless a Negro was placed in Hart's cabinet, and as Gibbs was considered the most able Negro in the State, he was invited to join Hart's administration. As superintendent, Gibbs was also president of the board of trustees of a proposed agricultural college. The manuscript records of Superintendent Gibbs demonstrate that he was intelligent and much interested in developing public education. . . . The public school system in Florida experienced rapid growth under the leadership of Gibbs, who was interested in education for all. . . .

Gibbs' sudden death at forty-eight on August 14, 1874, was a loss to the State and his race. . . .

Florida Negroes were also of considerable importance in the State legislature, though they were never in the majority. . . . Negro legislators were not always slavishly dependent on white Republicans. They demonstrated independence on several occasions, and frequently co-operated with Democrats in opposition to their own party, especially after 1870. Usually the freedmen were not too active on the house floor, though they were present for voting. A few of them, like Walls, played major roles in legislation and appeared to be at no disadvantage when dealing with their white opponents. Negro senators entered into debates on the floor more frequently than did members of the lower house. Walls, Charles H. Pearce, Robert Meacham, and John Wallace, in particular, refused to take a back seat to their white colleagues.

Education, economic security for the masses, relief and suffrage seemed to be of primary interest to the ex-slave lawmakers. Nearly all of them supported a public education system. Pearce and Henry S. Harman led the fight for a satisfactory school law. Freedmen supported the homestead law and other measures advantageous to the masses, white and Negro. Civil rights were also championed by the ex-slaves. Despite their reputed incapability, Negro legislators were a significant factor in Reconstruction politics and legislation. Some Negroes were not qualified just as some whites were not, but several of them were as able as the average white statesman in Florida before, during, and after Reconstruction.

Charges of widespread corruption made against Negro lawgivers are unsubstantiated. . . .

## GEORGIA: HENRY M. TURNER

*Henry M. Turner's greatest importance as a black leader was in the post-Reconstruction years, when, as a bishop of the African Methodist Episcopal Church, he became the most influential advocate of the back-to-Africa movement. This part of Turner's career is dealt with in detail in Edwin S. Redkey, Black Exodus: Black Nationalist and Back-to-Africa Movements, 1890–1910. In the following selection, which deals briefly with Turner's earlier life, Redkey suggests that his disillusioning experiences during Reconstruction were important in shaping Turner's later advocacy of emigration.*[16]

Bishop Henry McNeal Turner (1834–1915) was, without doubt the most prominent and outspoken American advocate of black emigration in the years between the Civil War and the First World War. By constant agitation he kept Afro-Americans aware of their African heritage and their disabilities in the United States. Turner possessed a dominating personality, a biting tongue, and a pungent vocabulary which gained him high office and wide audiences, first in Georgia's Reconstruction politics and later in the African Methodist Episcopal (A.M.E.) church. In his bitter disappointment with the American treatment of blacks, the bishop evolved an all-consuming nationalism which demanded emigration to Africa. To understand his forceful agitation in the years following 1890, one must know Turner's background and the nature of his vision of Africa.

Bishop Turner's life of nationalist agitation was founded on the frustrations of great energy and talent by the prejudice of white America. In South Carolina, where he was free-born, Turner

16. Edwin S. Redkey, *Black Exodus: Black Nationalist and Back-to-Africa Movements 1890–1910* (New Haven, Conn.: Yale University Press, 1969), pp. 24–27. Copyright © 1969 by Yale University. Reprinted by permission of the publisher.

experienced that prejudice from the beginning. He ran away from the cotton fields, where he had been apprenticed to work beside slaves, and found his own job sweeping out a law office. When the young law clerks observed his quick mind and eagerness to learn, they surreptitiously taught him to read and write, for legally no black was allowed to become literate. When he was twenty years old he was ordained a traveling evangelist in the white-dominated Southern Methodist church. Turner visited towns and cities throughout the South, preaching to both black and white. The prejudice he continually encountered made him ill at ease—resentful that he, a free man, should be prevented from doing all that his drive and ability suggested. His nascent nationalism found its first outlet in New Orleans, where, in 1858, he discovered something new to his experience—a church governed solely by blacks, the A.M.E. church. Without hesitation he joined it, partly as an act of defiance against whites and partly from attraction to an autonomous black organization in which he could realize his ambition for status and power.

During the Civil War years Turner found new scope for his energies and new hope for the Afro-American. When he had finished his training as a pastor in Baltimore, he was assigned to an important parish in Washington, D. C., on Capitol Hill. After the general emancipation he became openly belligerent and urged the newly freed slaves to defend themselves vigorously when attacked or insulted. Believing, furthermore, that blacks had not only rights but obligations, Turner agitated for the use of black troops by Union forces. After that became national policy, the first companies of black troops from Washington were mustered in his churchyard. As a reward for his recruiting efforts and in recognition of his leadership abilities, Turner was appointed chaplain to the black troops. His intense pride in his people had led him to dizzying new heights of personal achievement.

Turner's glory collapsed at the end of the war. Assigned to duty in Georgia as a chaplain with the Freedmen's Bureau, he soon found it impossible to remain in that government organization, which discriminated against him because of color. Turning to church organization he devoted his energies to establishing the A.M.E. church in Georgia where it had never before existed. Only in the black man's church, he thought, could he find freedom to lead and people to direct.

The Republican party, however, soon gave Turner another outlet for leadership and race pride. Because he was well known throughout the state and was already familiar with Republican officials in Washington, Turner was an obvious choice to become a party organizer among the freedmen of Georgia. He called the first Republican state convention and later was elected to the 1867 Georgia Constitutional Convention and the 1868 legislature. By organizing Loyal Leagues and Equal Rights Associations, he won the respect of blacks. By his participation in party and government affairs, he believed that at last he had also won the respect of whites. But like Adam cast out of the garden, Turner had tasted the forbidden fruit of political power, and no sooner had the state legislature convened than it sought to disqualify blacks from holding elective office. In a strong speech on the house floor, Turner protested the pending dismissal and demanded his rights as a free citizen of the United States. . . . But his fall was ordained and Turner was cast out.

Hoping to recover some of his prestige, he applied for the office of United States Minister to the black Republic of Haiti, but, failing in this, he asked for and received appointment as postmaster, at Macon, Georgia. As the first black postmaster in the state he became a *cause celebre,* but pressure mounted on the federal government for his dismissal, and Turner was charged with fraud, counterfeiting, and theft. After only two weeks in office he was dismissed. Thus, after three years of attempting to gain political power through the Republican party, Turner had to settle for an appointment as customs inspector for the "back waters around Savannah." Frustrated and without political power, he retreated into work for his black church, concluding that the United States was a white man's nation and that blacks must leave, preferably for Africa. . . .

## TWO VIEWS OF BLACK CONGRESSMEN

*In 1940,* The Negro in Congress 1870–1901, *by Samuel Denny Smith, was published. Smith's work embodies much careful research and contains important biographical information. But the spirit in which Smith deals with his subject is indicated by the foreword, written by J. G. De Roulhac Hamilton, a member of the Dunning school and the author of* Reconstruction in North Carolina. *After paying tribute to Dun-*

*ning's contributions to Reconstruction historiography, Hamilton says of Smith's book:*

> With careful and extensive use of all available sources, with balanced judgment, he has studied the lives and careers of an interesting group of men, who under no other conditions than those which prevailed in the South at the time, would ever have been found in the Congress of the United States. That South Carolina should be governed by recent laborers in its rice fields, and in the way so vividly portrayed by Pike in *The Prostrate State,* was no more remarkable than that Jefferson Davis should be succeeded in the Senate by Hiram Revels. Each fact excited thrilled approval in the North. The facts behind the fervid approval have been clearly described in the more general studies of the period; Dr. Smith has shown how little justification there was for it so far as the presence of the Negro in the hall of Congress was concerned. He has done so in an unbiased and scholarly fashion. . . .

> *Smith considered the black members of Congress supersensitive on the race issue and narrowly partisan; he decried their interest in civil rights, especially the Sumner Civil Rights Bill. He appeared to find their actions commendable only when they showed a conciliatory attitude toward former Confederates by favoring general amnesty measures. His conclusions and evaluations follow.*[17]

There are a number of conflicting opinions as to whether the Negro accomplished anything in Congress, and if not, why he failed. Negro historians and writers, such as [Carter G.] Woodson, [Alrutheus] Taylor, . . . are usually reliable in their facts, but their interpretations are not justified by the facts. They insist that no shortcomings of the Negro in politics are due to him, but always they are explained by the unfairness of the white man. On the other hand, white historians, writers, and statesmen, are almost a unit in agreeing that the Negro failed in Congress and that at least a part of the blame was inherent. It is proposed, therefore, to consider contemporary and later opinions, and to endeavor to reach an approximately accurate evaluation of the services of these Negro congressmen. . . .

17. Samuel Denny Smith, *The Negro in Congress 1870–1901* (Chapel Hill, N. C.: University of North Carolina Press, 1940), pp. viii–ix, 137, 143–44. Copyright © 1940 by the University of North Carolina. Reprinted by permission of the publisher.

From the data and facts examined, it seems clear that the Negroes failed to accomplish much worth while in Congress, during the period under survey. They were all race conscious and supersensitive, as was perhaps unavoidable under the circumstances. With some exceptions this resulted in a neglect of their white constituents. Further, they served to keep alive race friction, and they were used as a political football by Republicans, Northern Democrats, and even on occasions by Southern Democratic factions. The honors shown them in national conventions and in other places were for the purpose of controlling delegates and votes.

This study has attempted to prove that the Negroes who served in Congress from 1870 to 1901 were as a whole superior to those of their race who, with unfortunate results, took a contemporary part in local, county, and state government. It has been demonstrated in the introductory chapter that the Negroes in Congress from 1870 to 1901 were rather well equipped by education, previous political experience, and wealth, and that most of them had considerable white blood in their veins and were frequently aided by white friends. Therefore, much was expected of them as they had advantages most of their race did not have. Their lack of accomplishment was an argument that the Negro would do well, for a time at least, to forego political ambition in this realm and to confine his efforts to other vocations where he had a better chance of success.

*In* America's Black Congressmen, *published in 1971, Maurine Christopher covers much the same material as Samuel Denny Smith does. But she views the black Reconstructionists in a very different light. She attributes the absence of significant legislative achievements not to racial qualities, but to the small numbers and short tenure of the black congressmen of the Reconstruction era.*[18]

America's black congressmen have greatly enriched the nation's past by their talents, personalities, ideas, and accomplish-

18. Maurine Christopher, *America's Black Congressmen* (Thomas Y. Crowell Company, 1971), pp. 262–64. Copyright © 1971 by Maurine Christopher. Reprinted by permission of the publisher.

ments. Collectively their record is an inspiring example of what can be achieved in the face of immense difficulties.

In 1870, when Hiram R. Revels became a member of the United States Senate, the country was wracked by bitterness and turmoil in the aftermath of the Civil War. Despite this, hopes flourished for racial progress. Throughout the South, black Americans— many of whom had been slaves just a few years before—now held office as aldermen, sheriffs, judges, state legislators, and lieutenant governors. Revels himself seemed to be living proof that the war had substantially advanced the cause of human rights. Surely, it was thought, the Senate's acceptance of this black Mississippian showed that the federal government could be relied upon to force reluctant states of the old Confederacy to treat Negroes like other citizens.

Unhappily the aspirations of 1870 were not fulfilled. Revels and the blacks who followed him into Congress never had sufficient power to prevent the nullification of the reconstruction laws or of the Fourteenth and Fifteenth Amendments. Rarely did the first black members of Congress enjoy the mere luxury of being able to concentrate exclusively on the legislative job at hand. The simplest daily routines—traveling back and forth between their homes and Washington, for instance, or finding living accommodations in the capital—were struggles in a Jim Crow era. Campaigning was hazardous when Red Shirts and Ku Kluxers patrolled the polls to defeat Negroes and white liberals in the South.

Their limited resources were further drained by the protracted election challenges many black congressmen encountered in the House of Representatives. Elections were contested much more frequently during this period than they are today, and whites as well as blacks lost their seats, but these delaying tactics were especially damaging for men who had so little time to serve in Congress. The brevity of the two-year term in the lower house has frequently been criticized by political scientists on the grounds that a newcomer barely gets accustomed to his duties before he must run again. This truism was demonstrated to the point of absurdity in the case of some of these men, who were literally kept out of their seats until the campaign for the next Congress was already under way.

Even those black representatives who were repeatedly reelected lacked committee chairmanships or other power bases from which to bargain for their legislative proposals. Logically, as spokesmen for biracial constituencies that were important to the Republican party, they should have had political leverage. Despite this, the national Republican administration would not stand behind the Fourteenth Amendment when Revels warned that reconstruction would collapse in Georgia if that state were not barred from Congress until blacks were allowed to vote and hold office without harassment.

By 1876 it was obvious that the Republicans could not keep control of the White House without Negro support. Yet Senator Blanche K. Bruce and his white Republican allies were no more successful in saving the reconstruction government in Mississippi than Revels had been in Georgia. A special Senate investigating committee concluded that terror had been used to elect Democrats to state offices in 1875 and recommended that Mississippi be deprived of its congressional representation. When neither the President nor Congress challenged the results of that election, Bruce and Representative John R. Lynch must have realized that their party was doomed in Mississippi. Still the loyal black Republicans helped deliver the votes that elected Rutherford B. Hayes to the Presidency by a razor-thin margin in 1876.

All the while, Negro congressmen through their speeches were compiling a chilling chronological account of the atrocities perpetrated against blacks in the United States since the Civil War. In debate, Robert B. Elliott was masterly, as were Richard H. Cain, Josiah T. Walls, and James T. Rapier. Though they lacked the influence to get most of their bills passed, these first black congressmen did set visionary goals for the future with their proposals for aid to education, tax relief for the war-torn South, fair treatment for Indians as well as blacks, woman suffrage, economic protection for small farmers, and antilynching laws.

Their philosophies varied from man to man, but not one of them believed in separatism. To them common sense dictated that blacks and whites must cooperate if the nation was to achieve its highest potential. They kept reminding the majority race that the Constitution required that each person receive "equal protection of the laws," and they demanded that the nation make good on its written promises to its citizens. . . .

# Afterword

In spite of the fact that the total number of blacks registered to vote in 1867 slightly exceeded the number of whites, the power exercised by black voters was limited and, in most places, of brief duration. By 1874, white Redeemer regimes had been established in all of the former Confederate states except Mississippi, South Carolina, Louisiana, and Florida. In these states, where Republicans remained in power longest, blacks made up the vast majority of the Republican voters, but in no state did they receive offices or exercise political power commensurate with their numbers. When they first began to vote, inexperienced blacks tended to be diffident and ready to acquiesce in white leadership. As they gained experience and became politically more mature, however, they began to demand a larger voice in the Republican party and a larger share of the offices. Many whites regarded this as a threat of "Africanization." The growing assertiveness of the blacks caused whites to desert the Republican party and strengthened the determination of white "Redeemers" to resort to whatever means necessary to overthrow the Republicans and eliminate blacks from politics or dominate them completely.

Whites justified their lawless methods on the grounds that governments were "Negro-dominated" orgies of misrule, extravagance, and corruption. This version of Reconstruction and black Reconstructionists has long persisted. Even today, adequate studies of the actual workings of Reconstruction governments have not been made. But the charges of extravagance and corruption must be viewed in perspective. Under the new constitutions, states assumed added responsibilities, particularly in education and social services. Reconstruction state governments, like those in the North, also spent money on railroad subsidies. All this increased taxes, but tax rates in the South remained lower than in the North.

The question of corruption is more complex. That there was corruption is undoubtedly true, but this was not peculiar to the South. In the post-Civil War era, public morality was notoriously lax in the North—as witnessed by the scandals of the Grant administration and the Tweed Ring. By comparison, corruption in the South was on a small scale. Moreover, corruption in the South did not end with Reconstruction. Members of the Redeemer governments were also guilty of fraud and embezzlement. Some black Reconstructionists were venal and corrupt; some accepted bribes, perpetrated frauds, and were the henchmen of railroads and other groups seeking special favors from government; a few probably made substantial amounts of money by questionable or illegal methods; more profited on a petty scale. Other black Reconstructionists were incorruptible and took the lead in working for reform. In South Carolina state treasurer Cardozo "became the bane of every corruptionist's existence." Black Reconstructionists accused conservative whites of abdicating their responsibilities and using lawless violence to overthrow Republicans, rather than working with blacks to bring about reform. There was undoubtedly truth in Cardozo's assertion that Democrats did not want the reform efforts by blacks to succeed. Joel Williamson concluded that in South Carolina reform was largely achieved by the Republican government before the Democrats took over. Vernon L. Wharton concluded that the Republican regime in Mississippi "left a remarkable record of honesty." [1]

Certainly, some of the indictments and impeachments of black Reconstructionists were in the nature of political vendettas. Men like Cardozo, who were incorruptible, were charged along with men who were clearly guilty, and thus all blacks were discredited. After the Redeemer government came to power, Robert Smalls was convicted of taking a bribe and then immediately pardoned by the Democratic governor—thereby being prevented from vindicating himself by an appeal to a higher court.

For a century, black Reconstructionists have been under a cloud. Today, it appears that despite inexperience, lack of educational opportunities, and white prejudice, they made a creditable record. Black public officials were men of varying abilities. Some were remarkable natural leaders; black congressmen compared favorably in education and ability with their white counterparts; black administrators, such as Cardozo, Dunn, and Gibbs, were above reproach. Wright, the only black member of a state supreme court, was capable and honest. In more humble positions, as members of constitutional conventions and state legislatures, blacks made pos-

1. Joel Williamson, *After Slavery: The Negro in South Carolina During Reconstruction, 1861–1877* (Chapel Hill, N. C.: University of North Carolina Press, 1965), pp. 391, 397; Vernon L. Wharton, *The Negro in Mississippi, 1865–1890* (Chapel Hill, N. C.: University of North Carolina Press, 1947), p. 179.

sible the ratification of the Fourteenth and Fifteenth Amendments, and helped lay the foundations of the public school system in the South. Other objectives of black Reconstructionists—effective guarantees of universal suffrage, federal protection of civil rights, enforceable legislation prohibiting discrimination in places of public accommodations—were still being sought by their successors in the second Reconstruction, almost a hundred years later. In spite of subsequent efforts to malign and discredit them, black Reconstructionists left an important legacy that cannot be destroyed: they demonstrated the capacity of blacks to exercise the rights and responsibilities of citizenship, and helped win recognition of the dignity of all black Americans.

# Bibliographical Note

John R. Lynch was the only one of the black Reconstructionists to publish his memoirs. His first book, *The Facts of Reconstruction,* was published in 1913 and reprinted by Arno Press in 1969. In his later years, he revised and expanded this account. The later account, *Reminiscences of an Active Life: The Autobiography of John Roy Lynch,* edited by John Hope Franklin, was published in 1970 by the University of Chicago Press. A brief and fragmentary autobiographical sketch by Hiram R. Revels is in the Carter G. Woodson Collection in the Manuscript Division of the Library of Congress. None of the black leaders left any significant collection of personal papers. As sources of information on their careers and their views the scholar must rely on their published speeches, government documents, and newspapers.

The only full-scale, scholarly biography of a black Reconstructionist is Okon Edet Uya, *From Slavery to Public Service: Robert Smalls, 1839–1915* (London: Oxford University Press, 1971). An unpublished doctoral dissertation, "The National Career of Blanche Kelso Bruce," by Saide St. Clair (New York, N. Y.: New York University, 1947), deals mainly with the period from 1875 to 1898. *Respect Black: The Writings and Speeches of Henry McNeal Turner,* edited by Edwin S. Redkey (New York: Arno Press, 1971), contains a few of Turner's early speeches, but covers primarily the post-Reconstruction years. Mungo M. Pont's *The Life and Times of Bishop Henry M. Turner* (Atlanta, A. B. Caldwell Publishing Company, 1917) is uncritical and laudatory, and gives little information about the Reconstruction years. Merle M. Coulter, *Negro Legislators in Georgia During the Reconstruction Period* (Athens, Ga.: Georgia Historical Quarterly, 1968) is extremely hostile to Turner, but the author has uncovered some important source materials.

A few of the leading black Reconstructionists, including Revels, Bruce, John R. Lynch, Smalls, Pinchback, and Henry M. Turner, were included in the *Dictionary of American Biography* (22 vols., edited by Allan Johnson and Dumas Malone; New York: Charles Scribner's Sons, 1928–1944), the first volume of which was published in 1928.

The following biographical articles are to be found in the *Journal of Negro History*: G. Daniel Houston, "A Negro Senator [Blanche K. Bruce]," 7 (1922); Edward F. Sweat, "Francis L. Cardoza: Profile of Integrity in Reconstruction Politics," 46 (1961); Robert H. Woody, "Jonathan Jasper Wright, Associate Justice of the Supreme Court of South Carolina, 1870–1877," 18 (1933). Other biographical articles are: A. E. Perkins, "Oscar James Dunn," *Phylon* 4 (Second Quarter, 1943); N. W. Walton, "James T. Rapier, Congressman from Alabama," *Negro History*

*Bulletin* 30 (1967); Clifton H. Johnson, "Francis L. Cardoza: Black Carpetbagger," *The Crisis* 78 (September, 1971). Two books, both embodying
careful research and valuable biographical information, deal with black
congressmen: Samuel Denny Smith, *The Negro in Congress, 1870–1901*
(Chapel Hill, N. C.: University of North Carolina Press, 1940) and
Maurine Christopher, *America's Black Congressmen* (Thomas Y. Crowell
Company, 1971).

Studies of individual states contain important biographical information
and interpretations of black Reconstructionists. Pioneer studies were:
Alrutheus A. Taylor, *The Negro in South Carolina During Reconstruction*
(1924) and *The Negro in the Reconstruction of Virginia* (1926). Both
volumes were published by the Association for the Study of Negro Life
and History, Washington, D. C. Later studies are: Vernon Lane Wharton,
*The Negro in Mississippi 1865–1890* (Chapel Hill, N. C.: University of
North Carolina Press, 1947); Joe M. Richardson, *The Negro in the Reconstruction of Florida, 1865–1877* (Tallahassee, Fla.: Florida State University Press, 1965); and Joel Williamson, *After Slavery: The Negro in
South Carolina During Reconstruction, 1861–1877* (Chapel Hill, N. C.:
University of North Carolina Press, 1965).

*South Carolina During Reconstruction,* by Francis B. Simkins and
Robert H. Woody (Chapel Hill, N. C.: University of North Carolina
Press, 1932), was significant for its influence in initiating a reappraisal of
Reconstruction. Of the more general histories of Reconstruction the
two containing the most information on black Reconstructionists are:
W. E. B. Du Bois, *Black Reconstruction in America* (New York: Russell
and Russel, 1935; reprinted by Atheneum Press, 1969) and John Hope
Franklin, *Reconstruction after the Civil War* (Chicago, Ill.: University of
Chicago Press, 1961). *The Negro in Reconstruction,* by Robert Cruden
(Englewood Cliffs, N. J.: Prentice-Hall, Inc., 1969) includes little bio-
graphical material but contains helpful insights into the part that blacks
played in Reconstruction politics and government. *White Terror: The
Ku Klux Klan Conspiracy and Southern Reconstruction,* by Allen W.
Trelease (Harper & Row, Publishers, 1971), significantly presents over-
whelming evidence of the white opposition to black Reconstructionists
and the campaign of terror waged against them. *James Shepherd Pike:
Republicanism and the American Negro, 1850–1882,* by Robert Durden
(Durham, N. C.: Duke University Press, 1957), throws light on Pike's
racist views and the evolution of Reconstruction historiography.

# Appendix
# Biographical Sketches of
# Leading Black
# Reconstructionists

BRUCE, BLANCHE KELSO (March 1, 1841–March 17, 1898). The first black to serve a full six-year term in the U. S. Senate. Of largely white ancestry, born a slave in Prince Edward County, Virginia, son of an unknown white man and a house slave. As a boy, shared a tutor with his master's son. Taken at an early age with master's family to Missouri. Left master at outbreak of war. Tried unsuccessfully to enlist in Union army. Taught school in Missouri and Kansas, attended preparatory department of Oberlin College briefly, and worked on a Mississippi river boat. Settled in Mississippi at end of war, where taught school; acquired a plantation; entered politics. In 1870, named sergeant at arms of state senate; 1871, became tax assessor of Bolivar County; 1872, sheriff of Bolivar County. February, 1874, elected to U. S. Senate, where served from March, 1875 to March, 1881. As Senator, in addition to matters of immediate concern to blacks, showed special interest in improving navigation of the Mississippi, opposed exclusion of the Chinese, urged citizenship for Indians. Distinguished in appearance, polished in manner, maintained cordial relations with his white colleagues; worked in harmony with Democrat Lucius Q. C. Lamar, the fellow senator from Mississippi. Continued to be active in Republican politics after Reconstruction, dividing his time between Mississippi and Washington. In 1881, appointed by Garfield as Register of the Treasury; 1891–93, appointed by Harrison as Recorder of Deeds in Washington; 1897, appointed by McKinley as Register of Treasury, a position held until death.

CAIN, RICHARD HARVEY (April 12, 1825–January 18, 1887). Outstanding example of black Reconstructionist who combined roles of gospel minister and political leader. Born in Greenbrier County, Virginia, to free parents, a black father and a Cherokee Indian mother. Moved to Ohio at age of six. At 19, licensed to preach in Methodist Episcopal church, but discrimination against him because of his race soon caused him to join the African Methodist Episcopal church. 1860, attended Wilberforce University. 1861, assigned to church in Brooklyn, New York. 1865, assigned to South Carolina to do missionary work among freedmen and to found churches. Began publication of *Missionary Record,* which combined religion and support of the Republican party. His church in Charleston a stronghold of Republican political activity. Member of

South Carolina constitutional convention of 1868. 1868, elected to state senate. 1872, elected congressman-at-large. 1877, elected for a term as representative of second district. A vigorous, compelling orator; fought for Sumner Civil Rights Bill; effective in challenging, rebutting white racist congressmen. 1880, elected bishop; assigned to Louisiana and Texas. Helped to found Paul Quinn College; served briefly as its president. Became presiding bishop of district embracing northeastern states, a post held until death.

CARDOZO, FRANCIS L. (February 1, 1837–July 22, 1903). Minister, educator, and statesman. Born in Charleston, South Carolina, the son of a Jewish father who was editor of a Charleston newspaper, and mother who was half Negro, half Indian. After attending a Negro school in Charleston, sent abroad to attend the University of Glasgow and seminaries in Edinburgh and London. Ordained a Presbyterian minister; became pastor of Temple Street Congregational Church, New Haven, Connecticut, in 1861. 1865, sent by American Missionary Society to Charleston to work among freedmen. Established school that later became Avery Normal School. As chairman of education committee of constitutional convention of 1868, played important part in laying foundations of public school system of state. Elected secretary of state in 1868. 1872, elected state treasurer. In a period when many state officials were being charged with corruption, maintained a record of integrity; helped carry out financial reforms. Under the Redemption government in 1877, convicted of conspiracy to defraud—a charge that historians agree was politically motivated. Pardoned by Governor Wade Hampton. 1877, moved to Washington, D. C. 1884, became principal of Negro schools of Washington, a post held until death.

DUNN, OSCAR JAMES (c. 1821–November 20, 1871). First black elected to a high executive state office. Born a slave of pure black ancestry. Purchased while a boy by a firm of plasterers, who taught him the trade. Ran away when about 21 years old. Attained rudiments of an academic education and skill at playing violin. Enlisted in first regiment of black troops raised in Louisiana after New Orleans was occupied by Union forces; attained rank of captain. 1866, appointed member of Junior City Council of New Orleans. Active in founding Republican party in Louisiana. April, 1868, elected lieutenant governor with white carpetbagger Henry C. Warmoth as governor. Later, broke with Warmoth, whom he considered untrustworthy and too inclined to favor white conservatives. Appeared on way to gaining control of Republican party (over Warmoth) and becoming a potential candidate for governor and U. S. Senate, when he died suddenly before completing his term lieutenant governor.

ELLIOTT, ROBERT BROWN (August 11, 1842–August 9, 1884). Most able lawyer and one of most able orators and most influential politicians among black Reconstructionists. Claimed to have been born in Boston, Massachusetts, son of free parents, pure blacks from Jamaica; to have attended private schools; then to have gone to England, where attended High Holborn Academy, graduated from Eton College, studied law. Recent research casts doubt on these claims, but Elliott was a brilliant lawyer and orator. Moved to South Carolina at end of Civil War; in great demand as attorney; soon one of most powerful figures in Republican party. With his wife, a member of Rollin family, played a prominent part in the social life of Columbia and Charleston. Member of 1868 constitutional convention and of lower house of state legislature from July, 1868 to October, 1870. Appointed assistant adjutant general of state militia. Twice elected to Congress, in 1870 and 1872; both times resigned before end of term to return to South Carolina. In Congress, demonstrated ability as orator and knowledge of constitutional law. Defeated in bid for election to U. S. Senate in 1872. Elected again to lower house of state legislature, of which chosen speaker in 1875. 1876, Republican candidate for attorney general; claimed to be elected but ousted by the Hampton government in May, 1877. In post-Reconstruction period, returned to law practice. Moved to New Orleans, where died.

LYNCH, JOHN ROY (September 10, 1847–November 2, 1939). One of the most able and influential of black lawmakers and politicians; remained active in Republican politics long after end of Reconstruction. Born in Vidalia, Louisiana, child of a slave mother and a white father, whose sudden death prevented him from carrying out his intention of freeing his mother and her children. After father's death, family was sold and sent to Mississippi. Freed when Union troops occupied Natchez. Lynch, largely self-educated, learned photographer's trade. Campaigned for Republican party before old enough to vote. Appointed justice of peace of Natchez at age of 21. 1869, elected to state legislature where recognized as a leader and able parliamentarian. 1872, elected speaker of house. Next, elected to U. S. House of Representatives, where served from December, 1873 to March, 1877. Only Mississippi Republican congressman to survive Democratic sweep of 1875. Appealed in vain to President Grant to intervene in Mississippi to protect Republican voters. In Congress, supported Civil Rights Bill; condemned southern outrages, but maintained good relations with white members. Continued to be active in politics after Reconstruction, serving as chairman of Republican state central committee. 1882, reelected to Congress but defeated in 1884. Returned to Mississippi, where owned plantations. Appointed fourth auditor in Treasury Department by President Harrison. 1896, admitted to bar in Mississippi and Washington, D. C. 1898, appointed to a major of volunteers in Spanish American War. Later, served in regular army, retiring in 1911 with rank of major. Moved to Chicago, where admitted to bar; practiced law; continued to be interested in Republican politics. 1913, published *The Facts of Reconstruction* and articles in rebuttal of James Ford Rhodes' and Claude Powers' accounts of Reconstruction.

PINCHBACK, PINCKNEY BENTON STEWART (May 10, 1837–December 21, 1921). One of the most skillful and influential leaders among black Reconstructionists, although the highest offices eluded him. Son of William Pinchback, a white Mississippi planter, and Eliza Stewart, who was of mixed African, Caucasian, Indian ancestry. Free-born because his father had emancipated his mother; white in appearance; in later years, dressed elegantly; had the manners of a polished gentleman. 1846, sent to Cincinnati, where attended school. After death of his father in 1848, went to work on boats on Mississippi river. 1862, jumped ship; made way to New Orleans, which had been occupied by Union forces. Recruited troops for Corps D'Afrique, attained rank of captain. Helped organize Republican party; became member of state central committee. 1867, member of Louisiana constitutional convention. 1868, elected to state senate, where fought for a public accommodations law. 1869, opened a cotton factorage and steamship company; appointed by Grant register of land office of New Orleans. 1870–1881, published *New Orleans Louisianan*, a weekly. 1871, elected president pro-tempore of state senate; chosen lieutenant governor by vote of legislature on death of Oscar J. Dunn. Acting governor, December 9, 1872–January 13, 1873; while governor, Warmoth impeached. Aspired to nomination as governor in 1872, but accepted nomination as congressman-at-large. Claimed election, but never seated because Democratic opponent, who contested, was ultimately seated. Elected by legislature to U. S. Senate in January, 1873; but in March, 1876, finally denied seat. Embittered, turned to support of Democratic Governor Francis T. Nichols, in 1877. 1882, named customs surveyor of New Orleans. 1886, graduated from law department of Straight University; admitted to bar. 1890, moved to Washington, D. C., where lived until death.

REVELS, HIRAM RHODES (September 27, 1827–January 16, 1901). First black member of the U. S. Senate. Born in Fayetteville, North Carolina, of free parents of racially mixed ancestry. 1844, went to Indiana, where attended a Quaker academy. Later, attended schools in Darke County, Ohio and Knox College in Illinois. After being ordained a minister in the African Methodist Episcopal church, taught and preached at various places in Ohio, Indiana, Illinois, Kentucky, Missouri, Kansas. During Civil War, helped raise Negro regiments in Maryland and Missouri; and organized churches and schools among Mississippi freedmen. Settled in

Natchez after war; appointed alderman. 1869, elected to state senate. Entered politics reluctantly; always maintained a conciliatory attitude toward Southern whites. More a clergyman than a politician. Elected by Mississippi legislature to fill an unexpired term in U. S. Senate, where served from February, 1870 to March, 1871. Not aggressive as a Senator, but served with dignity. Favored legislation removing disabilities on Southern whites. Returned to Mississippi to help found and become first president of Alcorn University, the state college for Negroes. 1873, served briefly as secretary of state. Returned to Alcorn, but removed from presidency by Governor Ames. 1875, supported Democrats in campaign in which Republican carpetbag regime was overthrown. 1876, returned to Alcorn, but resigned because of ill health. Spent remainder of life in religious work, including ministerial posts at Holly Springs, Mississippi and Richmond, Indiana.

SMALLS, ROBERT (April 5, 1839–February 22, 1915). A hero of the Civil War and one of most powerful black politicians of Reconstruction era and after. Born in Beaufort, South Carolina, the son of a white father and house slave. Taken as a boy to Charleston, where hired out for work on the wharves and learned sailmaking and seamanship; learned to pilot a steamship before the age of 16. 1861, became pilot of the *Planter,* a transport steamer; May, 1862, delivered the *Planter* to the commander of the U. S. squadron blockading Charleston harbor. Served Union navy during remainder of Civil War. December 1, 1863, made captain of the *Pilot.* After the war, returned to Beaufort, where acquired extensive land holdings; engaged in business. Continued his education by receiving private instruction. Active in founding Republican party and initiating freedmen into politics. In a district with the highest ratio of blacks in the state, was sometimes known as "King of Beaufort"; but gained respect and support of some white constituents, working for their interests as well as those of blacks. 1868, member of state constitutional convention; elected to state house of representatives; elected to senate at next election. 1874, elected to Congress; reelected in 1876. 1877, convicted by redeemer government of accepting a bribe—a charge that was probably politically motivated; immediately pardoned by Governor Hampton. 1878, defeated for reelection to Congress, but elected again in 1880 and 1884. Defeated in 1886; continued to be active in Republican politics and to hold Beaufort in the Republican column. As member of 1895 constitutional convention, spoke out against disfranchisement of blacks. 1897, named customs collector at Beaufort, a post held until 1912.

WRIGHT, JONATHAN JASPER (February 11, 1840–February 18, 1885). Only black member of a state supreme court during Reconstruction. Born in Luzerne County, Pennsylvania, to parents who were of pure black ancestry and presumably free. Father was a farmer. Attended Lancaster University in Ithaca, New York. Taught school for a number of years; studied law in offices of white lawyers. 1865, sent by American Missionary Society to Beaufort, South Carolina, to organize schools for freedmen. 1866, returned to Pennsylvania to complete legal training and take legal examination (which he was permitted to take only after adoption of Civil Rights Act of 1866). First black to be admitted to bar in Pennsylvania. 1866, returned to Beaufort as legal adviser with Freedmen's Bureau; resigned in 1868. Elected to state constitutional convention of 1868 and to state senate; played important part in both bodies. February, 1870, elected by state legislature to fill a vacancy on the state supreme court. December, 1870, elected to a full six-year term on court. During term, wrote 87 opinions; showed competence as a lawyer. Retired from active politics in the post-Reconstruction period. Suffered from tuberculosis; died at Charleston at the age of forty-five.

# Index